Praise for *Eric Morecambe Unseen*:

'This affectionate and revealing book is sure to give a warm glow to anyone who dips into its potpourri of intimate memories. The real pleasure of this book is to be found in the extraordinary portfolio of photographs and memorabilia from his (Morecambe's) personal archive.' *Mail on Sunday*

'Delightful ... produces smiles of pure pleasure as soon as you open it.' Charles Spencer, *Sunday Telegraph*

'Cook paints a picture of a man of great gentleness and extraordinary talent ... here laid out in photos, letters and diaries. Sunshine indeed.' *Independent*

'A real sense of intimacy with a man who captivated millions in the great days of television.' *Sunday Express*

'A remarkable glimpse inside the mind and private life of Britain's best-loved comedian.' *Independent on Sunday*

William Cook

Morecambe and Wise Untold

HarperCollins*Publishers*

For My Mother

HarperCollins*Publishers*
77–85 Fulham Palace Road,
Hammersmith, London W6 8JB

www.harpercollins.co.uk

Published by HarperCollins*Publishers* 2012

A catalogue record of this book is available
from the British Library

ISBN 978-0-00-748829-2

MIX
Paper from
responsible sources
FSC˙ C007454

FSC™ is a non-profit international organisation established to promote
the responsible management of the world's forests. Products carrying the
FSC label are independently certified to assure consumers that they come
from forests that are managed to meet the social, economic and
ecological needs of present and future generations,
and other controlled sources.

Find out more about HarperCollins and the environment at
www.harpercollins.co.uk/green

CONTENTS

ACKNOWLEDGEMENTS

No need to read this bit unless you think you deserve a namecheck, and can be bothered to look for it in the list below. However, if you're determined to read on, here goes… Biography is a team game, no matter whose name goes on the cover, and all these people played a big part. Without their help, this book might still have been written, but almost certainly by someone else: my wife, Sophie, for letting me turn our home into an office; my children, Edward and Thea, for sharing a bedroom, so I could have a room in which to write; my agent, Gillon Aitken; my editor, Chris Smith; the book's designer, Terence Caven and everyone who took the time and trouble to answer a load of questions about a load of stuff that happened half a century ago: John Ammonds, Barry Band, Wyn Calvin, Pearl Carr, David and Pauline Conway, Alan Curtis, Ken Dodd, Bruce Forsyth, Michael Grade, Teddy Johnson, Sheila Mathews, Ernest Maxin, Eric Midwinter, Gail Morecambe, Gary Morecambe, Joan Morecambe, Patrick Newley, Phil Rose, Stan Stennett, Max Tyler, and Doreen Wise.

This book is a sort of sequel to *Eric Morecambe Unseen* (still available in a few good bookshops – and quite a lot of bad ones) which was also published by HarperCollins, and so it would be unfair – and rather rude – not to thank the two people who helped me most with that one: Julian Alexander and Ben Dunn. Thanks too to the *Guardian*, without whom I would have had to get a proper job – although I might still have to, if not enough people buy this book. Some of the stuff in here about Ken Dodd first appeared on the *Guardian*'s website, although if you've already come across it on the net, you must be even more of a comedy anorak than I am. The British Music Hall

Society helped too. If you're keen on that sort of thing (and if you've read this far, you must be) check out their house journal, *The Call Boy* — it's not as salacious as it sounds. And since I'm dishing out compliments, I really should finish off by thanking the person who taught me to read and write, and first took me to the theatre, the woman to whom this book is dedicated — my mum.

Eric: I've been in the army since I was
six years old.

Ernie: Impossible! You can't join the army at six.

Eric: Yes you can. I was in the infantry.

CHAPTER 1

RONNIE BARKER

IN 1983, A FEW MONTHS BEFORE HE DIED, Eric Morecambe sent a letter to his old friend Ronnie Barker. In 2005, a few months before he died, Ronnie Barker sent that letter on to me. I'd contacted Ronnie, the only comic who could hold a candle to Eric during the golden age of television, to ask him if he had any letters from Eric. Yes, replied Ronnie. He had a few. I was welcome to them. 'A very funny man,' he wrote. 'Good luck with the book.'

Most of the letters that Eric Morecambe wrote to Ronnie Barker were pretty perfunctory – short notes scrawled on the old calling cards Eric's mum had printed for him, when Eric was still a starstruck kid, looking for his first break in showbusiness. 'Master Eric Bartholomew', read the letterhead (this was long before he met Ernie Wise, and adopted his famous stage name). 'Vocal Comedy and Dancing Act, 43 Christie Avenue, Morecambe'.

It was intriguing to read these scribbled notes, from one star turn to another, but they didn't really amount to all that much. However there was one letter, utterly unlike all the rest, which almost jumped out of the pile. It was typed rather than handwritten, and the letterhead didn't read 'Eric Bartholomew, Vocal Comedy and Dancing Act'. It read 'Eric Morecambe, OBE'.

'Thanks for the old pound note,' wrote Eric Morecambe to Ronnie Barker, on 3 December 1983. 'I took it to the bank and they sent it to the police. It seems it was from a Post Office raid at North Allerton in 1936, so I presume they'll be getting in touch. I had a "funny turn" last week, ended up in hospital. As I was being wheeled in I thought, "Hell Fire, in the last five years I've been in more hospitals than theatres." Then I got to thinking.

'What's happened to showbusiness? When you look around, where is it going? I mean how can Les Dawson and Gene Kelly top the Royal Command Performance, eh? Gene Kelly looked better than Les Dawson and Gene Kelly's been dead for two years. Harry Secombe is now half of the invisible man. He tells me he's doing twenty-six God slots, and next year he and Thora Hird are opening their own Abbey. You had the right idea. Twelve months off and just doing adverts. I was back in hospital last week and as the doctor was thumping my chest I noticed he was wearing a Ronnie Barker watch.

I was with Frankie Howerd two weeks ago. He's got trouble with his legs so now he can only walk after little boys![1] Tommy Cooper's in a home in Eastbourne, but it was too expensive so he's gone into digs.[2] I heard that your little chap isn't too well. He has to lie down before he can get up. No, you had the right idea, twelve months off and just doing a few of those adverts.

I sat in my office this morning and looked around. What have I achieved? Honestly, what have I achieved in forty-four years in showbiz? A funny heart and a rich partner. I wouldn't mind if it had been the other way around. He said to me the other day we should cut the scripts down, so he took out two "Oh Really's" and a "Then What Happened?" All his lines.

'No, you had the right idea – twelve months off and a few of those adverts where you dress up as a woman and play yourself. Ah well. Thought you might find the enclosed letter interesting. Drop me a line sometime.'

*   *   *

It wasn't the longest letter I'd ever read, but it was one of the most revealing. This private correspondent was completely different from the Eric that we all knew (or thought we knew) on TV – that jolly everyman, laughing and joking in the corner of your living-room. This letter made me realize I didn't really know him after all. It was a letter from a frail and pensive man – doubtful of his achievements, mindful of his own mortality, weary of showbusiness and dismissive of his partner's talent. It was a letter from a man with only a few months left to live. And it made me realize that despite the sterling efforts of several biographers (especially Graham McCann, and Eric's son, Gary), there was another side to Morecambe & Wise, a side as yet untold.

Like millions of people, I grew up with Eric and Ernie. Like millions of people who never met them, I felt I'd known them all my life. We used to laugh at other comics – Dick Emery, Benny Hill, Mike Yarwood – but you never felt you really knew them. Even when they weren't dressing up or pretending to be other people, deep down you always knew they were putting on

Ronnie shares a joke with Eric and Ernie at the *That's Entertainment* film premiere, London 1974.

an act. Eric and Ernie were the only ones who really knew how to play themselves. J.B. Priestley said all great clowns look like people from another planet. Not Eric and Ernie. They looked like the boys next door. They were such naturalistic comics that their meticulously rehearsed routines seemed spontaneous and unscripted. In fact, they hardly seemed like comics at all. They were more like everyone's favourite uncles, cracking jokes at your sister's wedding, horsing around at your auntie's house on Boxing Day. But it takes a lot of work to make something look so easy, and no one worked harder than Morecambe & Wise. This letter hinted at the years of hard grind that went into creating that illusion – decades of monotonous toil which cut short Eric's life.

Ronnie Barker outlived Eric Morecambe by more than twenty years. Like Eric said, he had the right idea – twelve months off, apart from a few adverts. Eric never had twelve months off in his life. The longest he ever had was six months, and that was after his first heart attack. When he wrote that letter to

Ronnie Barker he was about to retire. He never got a chance. A few months later, he accepted an invitation from his old Variety colleague Stan Stennett to do a show at the Roses Theatre in Tewkesbury, had a heart attack in the wings, after his sixth curtain call, and died in hospital that night. He was fifty-eight.

Three years after Eric's death, when Ronnie Barker was fifty-seven, his doctor warned him that showbusiness was jeopardizing his health. Like Eric, Ronnie Barker had never been in more demand. Unlike Eric, he retired immediately, enjoyed nearly twenty years of retirement, and lived until he was seventy-six. Forty-four years of showbiz was what killed Eric Morecambe. So, to answer his own question, during those forty-four years, what had Eric and Ernie achieved?

It's such an obvious question that nobody but Eric could have asked it. But the fact that he saw fit to ask it, of himself and Ronnie Barker, says an awful lot about the lifelong self-doubt and insecurity that drove him on, and on. The most important thing that Eric and Ernie achieved was happiness, of course — millions of happy memories that live on in the minds of millions of people they never met. But they achieved something else as well, and I didn't realize what it was until Ronnie Barker died.

Ronnie Barker was a comic actor, not a comedian. His comedy was confined to sitcoms, sketches and plays. His partnership with Ronnie Corbett was one of TV's greatest double acts, but *The Two Ronnies* didn't end up on TV — they started there. When you saw them on TV, you were watching the whole story. They'd been brought together for *The Frost Report*, then given their own TV series. After *The Two Ronnies*, they went their separate ways.

Morecambe & Wise, on the other hand, were a classic front-of-curtain double act. What we saw on TV was merely the end of a long and very windy road. We loved them because they'd spent a lifetime learning how to make a live audience love them, in an endless success of live shows. Eric and Ernie honed their act onstage, in pantomime and summer season. They played circus tents, seaside piers, even nude revue. They teamed up when they were teenagers, and they were still together forty years later. More than any other double act, it really was like a marriage — 'an English marriage,' as John Mortimer put it, 'missing out on the sex, as many English marriages do'.[3] And unlike a lot of English marriages, it really was for richer or poorer, until death us do part. They'd been together for over ten years before they landed their own TV series, and another ten before they became proper TV stars. Even then, it was ten more years before they really hit the big time, in a TV show that harked back to all those Variety theatres, long since demolished, where they'd learnt their trade. I didn't know it at the time, and nor did any other youngsters who were watching, but when we sat down to watch *The Morecambe and Wise Show* on TV, we were really watching a tongue-in-cheek tribute to the lost world of Variety – a uniquely British brand of Light Entertainment whose origins went all the way back to Victorian music hall.

'There's no real comparison with the old theatres,' said Ernie, towards the end of his career, after he and Eric had settled into a comfortable routine of pre-recorded TV shows. 'They were designed for relationships between artists and audience, and you can actually feel that contact. They were built for the sort of sound that today's entertainers, who depend on microphones, just can't understand. In those old theatres your voice could hit the back wall and you'd hear it bounce back. That's something Eric and I appreciate.'[4] Even after all those years, they still missed the old red plush and gold.

Eric and Ernie's studio set had wings and curtains, just like a proper theatre. It even had a wooden stage, which clunked when you walked about on it. Unlike other TV stars, they didn't play to the camera. They played to the studio audience, giving viewers the feeling they were eavesdropping on a theatre show. 'All we have done is adapt music hall on television,' Ernie told the *TV Times*. Television was the deluge which washed away the old music halls, and their TV show was like a Noah's Ark of live Variety. When Rubenesque actress Janet Webb came on to take a bow, having played no previous part in the proceedings, fans of George Formby would recall how his rotund wife Beryl would gatecrash his curtain calls at Blackpool Opera House. 'You're making us look like a cheap music-hall act,' Ernie used to complain, in mock protest. 'Well, we are a cheap music-hall act,' Eric would reply.

'We came in at the end of the music-hall era,' said Ernie, a few years before Eric died, 'and we were young enough to start again in a new medium, television.'[5] Yet Eric and Ernie spent the best years of their lives in Variety. By the time they made their first successful series for the BBC, they were already in their forties, with thirty years in showbusiness behind them. That thirty-year stint, from the Blitz to the Beatles, was a never-ending treadmill of live shows. This was where their act evolved, at the bottom of long-forgotten bills, alongside long-forgotten entertainers – jugglers, trapeze artists, ventriloquists, contortionists, even performing animals. Sure, it was a slog, but it was also a priceless apprenticeship. There's nothing like it nowadays.

Those live Variety shows really were fun for all the family. They weren't only fun for office parties or stag and hen nights, like so many comedy shows nowadays. Today live comedy is booming, but a lot of the shows are really only suitable for lads and lasses on the pull. Variety taught Eric and Ernie how to play to mums and dads and grandparents and grandchildren – all at the same time. That's why three generations used to sit around the television to watch them, just like they used to sit together in the stalls.

It was this broad reach which made the *Morecambe and Wise Christmas Show* a national institution, but Eric and Ernie didn't acquire that broad reach on TV. They acquired it in countless Christmas pantomimes, and at the end of an endless succession of seaside piers. Max Bygraves described an audience as 'a group of people in danger, frightened and anxious for someone responsible to take charge'.[6] Eric and Ernie knew all about the danger of live theatre, and they knew exactly how to put anxious audiences at their ease. Their childlike charm was what made them great, and they acquired this charm in Variety, playing to family audiences in family shows. Timeless and ageless, daft and endearing, that's why their old routines still feel so fresh today.

So what was it really like, that lost world they came from? How did it shape them? What were the other acts like? And the theatres? And the shows? Why did Eric and Ernie survive, while so many other Variety acts vanished? What were they like before they were famous, before Eric Bartholomew and Ernest Wiseman became Morecambe & Wise? 'What's happened to showbusiness?' asked Eric, in his last letter to Ronnie Barker. 'What have I achieved?' This book isn't about Eric and Ernie's TV triumphs. It's a book about the places where those triumphant shows evolved. It's the story of the spit and sawdust circuit where they refined their comic craft, and polished it, and polished it, and finally became the greatest double act that Britain has ever seen.

CHAPTER 2

ERIC BARTHOLOMEW

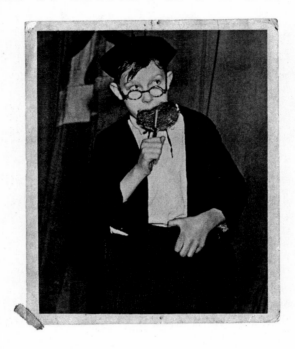

IN 1973 ERIC AND ERNIE'S MANAGER, Billy Marsh, gave his most famous clients a present. It was a reel-to-reel film of their perennial live show. Ever since Eric's first heart attack, in 1968, after a late-night show at Batley Variety Club, Eric and Ernie had cut back on their live commitments and focused on TV instead. But although they'd packed in pantomime and summer season, they'd been a live act for far too long to forsake the theatre completely, so instead of long runs in Variety clubs, they now limited their live work to occasional one-night stands in concert halls. These shows were so lucrative that they called them bank raids. 'You've just seen thirty years go by before your very eyes in one hour's performance,' they used to tell these audiences, after they'd performed the live act they'd been honing throughout their adult lives. Thankfully in 1973, at the Fairfield Halls in Croydon, Billy Marsh was wise enough to preserve this piece of history on film.

One man who was lucky enough to be there that night was Patrick Newley, editor of *The Call Boy*, the journal of the British Music Hall Society, and a sometime comic too. 'We always took the TV shows for granted,' says Patrick. 'When I first saw them live, in 1973 at the Fairfield Halls in Croydon, they blew me away. I just could not believe it.' This isn't the opinion of a blinkered fan. Patrick had always liked Morecambe & Wise, but he never stayed in to watch them on telly. It was only because someone gave him a ticket that he went along. He was glad he'd gone. 'When you saw Morecambe & Wise it was electrifying onstage. They blew you away with their timing. The whole atmosphere in the audience, it was incredible. And the love that came over the footlights – both ways – was extraordinary. As I say, we took it for granted on TV. A couple of older people have told me they saw Laurel and Hardy live when they came over to Britain in the Fifties, and audiences just went barmy – it didn't matter what they did. They just went crackers. That's what it was like watching Morecambe & Wise.' They even made the band laugh. By the end of the evening, Patrick had become an ardent fan. 'They were idols, and there they were – actually in front of us. You could reach out and almost touch them. It was like one great big party. You held on to every word they said.' It didn't feel like an act at all. It felt like talking to old friends. 'They were completely for real,' says Patrick. 'You didn't think that there was anything contrived there. It wasn't as if they were doing a set routine.' But they were. It was a classic hour of knockabout, worn smooth by repetition, and its origins stretched right back to the beginning of the Second World War.

The first time that Eric and Ernie set eyes on one another was in a cinema in Manchester, where the bandleader and impresario, Jack Hylton, was holding auditions for his latest 'discoveries' show. It was August 1939, a few weeks before war broke out. Eric and Ernie were both just thirteen years of age, but there was a world of difference between them. For while Eric was up onstage, auditioning alongside a host of other hopeful amateurs, Ernie was already a paid-up professional, sitting alongside Hylton in the stalls.

Eric's father, George, and work mates on road duty. They called themselves 'The Follies'.

Eric had come down from Morecambe with his mother Sadie, a kindly but ambitious woman, determined to do her best for her only child. Eric's parents were a happy couple, but they could hardly have been less alike. Unlike Eric's mum, Eric's father George was breezy and unambitious. A calm and amiable fellow, he worked for the local council, chiefly as a manual labourer, from the day he left school until the day that he retired. Eric's mum, conversely, never stopped striving for something better. Born in an era when few working-class women were able to acquire a decent education, she slaved away in a variety of unskilled jobs, from cleaning to waitressing, and whatever she lacked in qualifications, she more than made up for in wit and drive.

John Eric Bartholomew was born on 14 May 1926 ('If my father hadn't been so shy I could have been two years older') and at first it looked as if he'd take after his dad. Like his dad, he enjoyed fishing and football more than school. 'I wasn't just hopeless in class,' he confessed, cheerfully. 'I was terrible.' 'He was no student,' confirmed Sadie. 'His school reports were our despair.'[1] When she offered to pay for private education, Eric's headmaster told her it would be money down the drain. Not that Eric was remotely bothered. 'I had no bright ambitions,' he said. 'To me, my future was clear. At fifteen I would get myself a paper round. At seventeen I would learn to read it. And at eighteen I would get a job on the Corporation like my dad.'[2]

Yet there was one thing Eric was good at, and that was performing. As soon as he could walk, he was dancing to his mum and dad's gramophone records. From the age of three he was doing song-and-dance routines for relatives and neighbours – not just nursery rhymes, but grown-up ballads like 'Blue Moon'. When he was ten, Sadie enrolled him in a local dance class, at a shilling a lesson. He was the only boy in the class, but Sadie made him stick at it, and soon he was entertaining pensioners in church halls for plates of pies and peas. When his teacher told Sadie that her son showed promise, she went out charring to pay for private lessons, at half a crown a time, and thanks to her dedication and self-sacrifice, Eric's dancing flourished. His teacher paired him up with a local girl aged twelve called Molly Bunting (she'd be in her early eighties now) and the schoolboy crush he had on her did his dancing no harm at all. They danced Fred Astaire and Ginger Rogers style to tunes from the Hollywood musicals that were all the rage in the local cinemas: 'Cheek To Cheek', 'Let's Face The Music And Dance', 'Smoke Gets In Your Eyes'. When his parents took him to the Jubilee Club at Torrisholme, a few miles from home, the social secretary asked George how much money Eric charged to do a turn. 'He'll do it for nothing,' said George. Sadie was aghast. In the end, they agreed on five shillings. It was Eric's first paid gig. Soon, Eric was playing local working men's clubs as far afield as Preston, performing every Saturday lunchtime and dinnertime for up to a pound a time. At the age of twelve, he was already earning more in two days than his dad made in a week.

Today Morecambe is a sleepy, slightly melancholy place, a resort for bird-watchers rather than aspiring entertainers, but when Eric was a lad it was a bustling holiday destination, the self-styled 'Naples of The North'. Noel Coward stayed at the Midland Hotel, one of the finest art deco buildings in the country, and the Winter Gardens (where Eric's mum and dad met) staged all the top Variety acts. Built in 1898 by Frank Matcham, the doyen of Variety architects, this was one of Britain's biggest Variety theatres, with nearly 3000 seats. It was here at this palatial theatre (still there, just about, but shut down and derelict awaiting restoration, having been saved by local enthusiasts) that

Eric saw Bud Flanagan and Chesney Allen, the finest double act of their day. Flanagan and Allen were one of the few duos whose humour was based on affection rather than irritation. This show planted a seed that grew. Affection would be the kernel of Eric and Ernie's act. Afterwards, Eric waited at the stage door for Flanagan and Allen's autographs. He subsequently incorporated impressions of both men into his own fledgling routine.

Eric didn't just do impressions. He started singing in the seafront hotels, for a local bandleader called Billy Baxter, and entered talent contests on the front, run by a concert party called The Nigger Minstrels (in those days, the word 'nigger' was not regarded as derogatory – well, not in the music halls, at least). The other contestants were all grown-ups, but they were only amateurs. Eric was a budding pro. After he'd won three years running, he was disqualified. His success was discouraging genuine holidaymakers from joining in.

At the age of thirteen, Eric was already getting too big for Morecambe, so Sadie started taking him further and further afield. In 1939, she entered him for a talent contest in Hoylake, a seaside town in far-flung Cheshire, a few

On Morecambe pier. *Left to right:* Sadie, Eric, Arthur Tolcher's mum, a veteran music hall entertainer, and an unknown friend. Arthur would find fame many years later as the harmonica player who never got to finish his tune... 'Not now, Arthur!' became their catchphrase.

Two rare glimpses of Eric's earliest attempt in show business, here performing his 'I'm not all there' routine.

CONFIRMATION COPY

JACK HYLTON'S THEATRICAL AGENCY LIMITED.

Licensed Annually by London County Council   Members of the Agents' Association Ltd.

Telephone : Gerrard 2474-5-6 & 2255   ASTORIA HOUSE
Telegrams : " Jaxback, Lesquare, London."
Cablegrams : " Jaxback, London."   62 SHAFTESBURY AVENUE
                    Entrance in Wardour Street   LONDON. W.1

This Agency is not responsible for any non-fulfilment of contracts by Proprietors, Managers or Artistes.

No. *net*

An Agreement made the ___21st___ day of ___august___ 19 41

BETWEEN ___Jack Hylton Bands Ltd___ (hereinafter called " the Management ")

of the one part and ___"Morecambe"___ (hereinafter called " the Artiste ") of the other part, *Witnesseth* that the Management hereby engages the Artiste

and the Artiste agrees to present / appear as ___directed by Mr. Bryan Michie___

(or in his usual entertainment) at the Theatre, and from the dates for the periods and at the salary stated in the Schedule hereto, upon and subject to the terms and conditions of Schedule 1. of the Ordinary Form of Contract contained in the Award of Mr. A. J. Ashton, K.C. dated 22nd September, 1919.

SCHEDULE

One week at ___Liverpool Empire___ commencing ___25th August___ 19 41
One week at ___Edinburgh Empire___ commencing ___1st September___ 19 41
___ week at ___ commencing ___ 19 ___
___ week at ___ commencing ___ 19 ___

The artiste agrees to appear at ___12___ Evening / ___1___ Matinee performances per week at a salary of

£ : :
£ : :
£ 7. : NET.

FOR PRODUCTION OR COMBINATION BOOKINGS:

___ to receive as remuneration ___

of the gross door receipts less deduction of entertainment tax ___

THE ARTIST SHALL IF REQUIRED BY THE MANAGEMENT, APPEAR IN ANY BROADCAST PERFORMANCE WITHOUT EXTRA FEE.

THE THEATRE COMPANY MAY CLOSE THE THEATRE IN THE EVENT OF AIR RAIDS OR WARNINGS. ARTISTS SHALL BE PAID FOR ANY PERFORMANCES NOT PLAYED IN RESPECT OF SUCH CLOSURE.

for & on behalf
JACK HYLTON BANDS
Signature ___
Address ___

J. COLLARD, Printer, 24 Litchfield Street, London, W.C.2

Eric's first contract of employment, with theatre impresario Jack Hylton.

hours away by train. Eric sang a song called 'I'm Not All There', while licking an enormous lollipop. With his half-mast trousers and sock suspenders, the target audience for his winsome act was doting aunts and grannies, rather than adolescent boys and girls. No wonder Eric felt so ambivalent about showbusiness. He loved to lark about, but he hated dressing up.

Eric duly won this talent contest, just like he'd won all the others, but he felt even more ambivalent than usual when he was presented with his prize. His only reward for this fancy-dress ordeal was another fancy-dress ordeal – an audition for someone called Jack Hylton. 'I felt my prize was a complete swizz,'[3] he said, but Sadie realized this award was far more valuable than some tinplate trophy. When Hylton came to Lancashire, Eric was summoned to appear before him, which is how he ended up on the makeshift stage of a Manchester cinema, wearing a beret and a bootlace tie.

Eric sang 'I'm Not All There', but he soon realized Hylton wasn't so easy to please as the mums and dads of Morecambe. 'OK,' said the master showman. 'What else?' Fortunately, Eric had a few more routines up his sleeve. He put on a battered straw hat and a mangy fur coat to mimic Bud Flanagan singing 'Underneath The Arches'. Then he changed into top hat and tails to imitate Fred Astaire. Finally, he blacked up to play G.H. Elliott, 'the chocolate-coloured coon' (it seems bizarre today, but there was nothing remotely risqué about blacking up back then – Al Jolson, who'd blacked up as *The Jazz Singer* in the first 'talkie', was one of Hollywood's biggest stars).

At last, Hylton showed a flicker of interest. 'Your boy has talent,' he told Sadie. 'Maybe we can use him. We'll let you know.' To Sadie, it sounded a lot like 'don't call us, we'll call you'. As she licked her hanky and wiped away Eric's make-up, she relayed Hylton's ambiguous appraisal to her son. Eric was sure he'd blown his big chance, but unlike Sadie, he couldn't have cared less. 'I felt a right Charlie, dressing up and putting on rouge, lipstick, eyebrow pencil and that nigger minstrel make-up, which I knew was still round the back of my ears going home to Morecambe on the bus.'[4] He barely gave a second thought to the lad he'd seen sitting beside Hylton. Eric and Ernie had set eyes on one another, but they hadn't exchanged a word.

Above **A wonderful moment when Eric was, for once, caught off guard.**

Right **Eric's earliest interest was in photography. He once took a box brownie to a camera shop to have the film developed and was kept by staff eager to see such an antique!**

CHAPTER 3

ERNEST WISEMAN

Photo : Savoy Studios.
ERNEST WISEMAN.
(The Clown).

ERIC'S TRIP TO MANCHESTER was really nothing out of the ordinary. Variety was booming, juvenile shows were all the rage, and impresarios like Jack Hylton needed a constant influx of fresh talent. Ernie, on the other hand, had arrived in Manchester by a far more extraordinary route. Born in East Ardsley, near Leeds, on 27 November 1925, six months before Eric, Ernie's childhood was a lot tougher than Eric's. Money was tight in Eric's home, but Sadie made sure he never went without, while Ernie's mum had to scrimp and save for every penny. This was partly because she had five children to look after, but it was mainly because her husband was a hopeless spendthrift. 'He was a nice man, a very generous man,' remembered Ernie, half a century later. 'He didn't have much money, but he was always very generous with what he had.'[1] Sadly, these decent attributes, which made him a fine friend and such an affectionate father, didn't make him a terribly reliable bread-winner, leaving Ernie with a lifelong dread of poverty and debt.

Ernie's mum and dad had the sort of romance you read about in kitchen-sink novels. His mother, Connie, was a weaver. His father, Harry, was a railway porter. They met on a tram (he tripped over her umbrella) and fell in love at first sight. Connie's dad was relatively well-to-do, and he thought that Harry was way below his daughter's station. He told Connie that if she married him he'd cut her off without a penny. Naturally this threat drove her straight into Harry's arms, but even when the happy couple moved into a rented room together, Connie's dad didn't waver. The only thing she was allowed to take with her was her piano, which she'd saved up to buy from the five shillings she put away every week while working in the woollen mills.

Connie played the piano beautifully, and this instrument became a talis-man for Ernie's showbiz ambitions. It ensured that there was always music in his home, even when there was precious little else. 'I think now of that piano as the focal point of the home, occupying pride of place in the kitchen with the whole family grouped around it singing songs together,'[2] he recalled, some sixty years on. What's more, it was a constant reminder that prudence was the key to the good things in life. 'When there's no money in the house, love flies out the window,' Connie used to warn him. 'Save a little, spend a little and remember that your bank book is your best friend.' That piano proved her point. She'd toiled for ten years in the mills to buy it, from the age of thirteen, three days after she left school. If she hadn't saved up for that piano, would Ernie have become a showman? And would he have managed his showbiz career with such financial nous? Eric always took the mickey out of Ernie's careful way with money, but like a lot of jokes this put-down was really a backhanded compliment. Deep down, Eric knew the thrift that Ernie had learnt from Connie was central to their joint success.

Ernie's dad didn't have the first idea about saving money, but he did know how to put on a show. While Connie was content to play the piano in the privacy of her own parlour, Harry was a proficient part-time showman, and at weekends he earned a few extra bob doing song-and-dance routines in local working men's clubs. As Ernie said, he would have made a perfect Redcoat. Connie taught her son to sing, Harry taught him to tap-dance, and at the age of seven he joined his dad onstage in a duo called Carson and Kid.

Unlikely you would go to Bradford with a show such as this, which included Ernie when it was performed at the Bradford Alhambra, but back in 1936 the times were less enlightened.

Ernie's costume was just as daft as Eric's — red clogs, a loud checked suit, a bootlace tie and a bowler hat without a brim. However, unlike Eric, he didn't mind a bit. Soon Ernie and his dad were gigging every Saturday and twice on Sundays, catching the last bus home at ten o'clock on Sunday night, with Ernie fast asleep on his dad's shoulder. Ernie had found his true vocation, and forty years later he could still recall this netherworld in almost microscopic detail: 'There'd be a snooker room and a place where you played darts. There'd be fruit machines. There'd be beer and sandwiches, pies, potato crisps, pickles and bottles of tomato sauce, the whole place crowded for the concert with working-class people in their Sunday best. The men wore blue serge suits, white shirts with detachable, boned collars and patterned ties fastened to the shirt front by a clip, pocket handkerchiefs to match, black shoes and short hair slicked down. The women and girls wore homemade dresses, their hair in tight curls still smelling faintly of heated tongs, and the bolder, unmarried ones wore make-up. There'd be a scattering of children running about, getting in the way of waiters in white coats and long white aprons carrying trays laden with drinks, mainly beer. If they were paid with a note, you'd see them holding it in their teeth till they had produced the change.'[3]

Soon they started getting bookings out of town, which meant they sometimes didn't get home until the small hours. Inevitably Ernie found it hard to stay awake at school, and inevitably his school work suffered. Harry was breaking the law, and he knew it — and as Carson and Kid prospered, the local education authority stepped up their efforts to put this illegal double act out of business. If Ernie had been as diffident about performing as Eric, the authorities would have had a point. However Ernie loved every minute of it, and Harry couldn't afford to stop. Thanks to his son, he was making more money in the clubs at weekends than he made on the railway during the working week. When the inspectors stopped them performing in Leeds, they went to Wakefield. When the inspectors stopped them performing in Wakefield, they went to Bradford. Eventually the inspectors gave up, and left Carson and Kid alone.

Even in those early days Ernie must have had bags of star quality, since there was nothing terribly unusual about the actual content of the act. The dialogue consisted of random snatches of mildly risqué crosstalk, shamelessly filched from more established double acts, and the songs were all familiar standards, made popular by professional entertainers. They were all pretty sentimental, and the one that really brought the house down was an especially slushy Al Jolson ballad called 'Little Pal'. Like Jolson, Harry would black up (was there anyone in those days who didn't?) and sing this sentimental song to Ernie, perched upon his knee: 'Little pal, if daddy goes away, if some day you should be on a new daddy's knee, don't forget about me little pal.' Ernie would reply: 'If some day I should be on a new daddy's knee, don't forget

A young Ernest Wiseman makes his mark on stage in Arthur Askey's *Bandwagon* show in 1939.

about me little pal.' This maudlin duet was a reliable tearjerker, and it was even more poignant in the light of what came to pass. Little did they know it, but 'Little Pal' would prove to be remarkably prophetic. However it wasn't Ernie's daddy who went away. It was his little pal, Ernie.

In 1938 a man called Bryan Michie came to Yorkshire, looking for new faces for Jack Hylton's latest juvenile revue. One of Britain's foremost band-leaders, Hylton was also a renowned impresario, and when Harry heard that Michie was holding auditions at the Leeds Empire, he sent Ernie along. For most kids this would have been terrifying. For Ernie it was a breeze. He cracked a few jokes, sang a song and finished off with a quick clog dance. 'I'm acting like a clown,' he sang, 'in this little one-horse town.' How could Michie refuse him? Nevertheless, like Eric, he was told to wait and see.

During the months that followed, Ernie did his best to keep busy. When the BBC came to Leeds to record a local talent show, he sang his party piece, 'Let's Have A Tiddly At The Milk Bar', and got two guineas for his trouble. He also took part in the *Nignog Revue*, an annual charity show at the Bradford Alhambra (Ernie was the only performer who got paid, since his family were so hard up, yet during his first few years in showbusiness he still managed to salt away more than £100). Finally, after months of waiting, a letter arrived from Jack Hylton, inviting Ernie down to London for an audition. The day Ernie's life turned upside-down was Friday 7 January 1939.

'Even now,' said Ernie, half a lifetime later, 'that thrilling succession of events has a fairytale quality.'[4] Indeed as rags-to-riches stories go, it would have seemed improbable even in a Hollywood musical. On Friday morning, Ernie and Harry caught the train from Leeds to London. On Friday afternoon, Ernie auditioned for Jack Hylton, in his office above the Princess Theatre. On Friday evening, Ernie appeared on the stage of the Princess Theatre, in a West End show called *Band Waggon*. Arthur Askey was top of the bill but Ernie stole the show. He spent the night at the Shaftesbury Hotel, the first hotel he'd ever stayed in, in a room with a light that went off and on when you opened and closed the toilet door. When Ernie saw that toilet light, he knew he had arrived. Back home, he always used to sing whenever he was on the loo. He had to. It was outside, and there was no lock on the door.

A very early still of Ernie, long before Eric could quip, 'You can't see the join!'

The front-page headlines in the morning papers were even more exciting: 'Railway Porter's Son Star Overnight'. Hylton promptly put Ernie on a three-year contract at £6 a week — three times his father's weekly wage. He offered Harry a contract too, but mindful of his wife and family, and his steady job back home, Harry turned him down. Throughout his life, Ernie remained convinced his dad had made the wrong decision. 'Much later, Mum told me that going back without me was the break-

ing of him. I was the closest to him, I had been his constant partner and now that I had disappeared from the scene he had no heart to go on performing. He tried to bring on the other kids a bit, but they never showed the same aptitude as I had and in the end he gave up trying.'[5] Don't forget about me little pal, indeed.

After a week of lavatorial luxury at the Shaftesbury Hotel, Ernie moved into a flat above an Italian restaurant in St Martin's Lane. His flatmates were two other child stars in the same show, Maureen Flanagan and Maureen Potter (who later became a celebrated actress and comedienne in her native Ireland) and their chaperone, Mrs Rodway, who looked after Ernie's wages. Thirty-five years later he could still recite the figures. 'She sent three pounds home, paid twenty-five shillings for my digs and meals, which she cooked, gave me five shillings a week spending money and banked the rest.'[6]

Like Ernie, Hylton was a northerner who'd escaped his poor beginnings as a young performer (he'd started out playing the piano in pubs in Bolton) and in Ernie he clearly saw something of the boy he'd once been. They even shared the same fondness for traditional northern food (as opposed to fancy foreign muck) and Hylton would often invite Ernie into his dressing-room to share a plate of cold tripe or a pork pie – delivered to him every week from a butcher in Bolton. 'He was a typical Lancashireman,' said Ernie, fondly. 'Very down to earth. Always picking his nose and scratching his arse.'[7] In between picks and scratches (and pork pies and plates of tripe) Hylton cast an expert eye over Ernie's nascent act. He whittled down his surname (from Wiseman to Wise), traded in his northern clogs for southern tap shoes, and replaced his beaten-up old bowler hat with a smart straw boater. In his dapper new dinner suit, Ernie was now a song-and-dance man, not a clown. He would remain a song-and-dance man, rather than a clown, throughout his life.

When *Band Waggon* closed, a few months later, Hylton took his own band on tour. He took Ernie with him. Mrs Rodway came too, to make sure he was out of the theatre by ten o'clock, as the law required. The law also required him to go to school every day, but since the show was in a different town each week he never learnt that much. He generally sat at the back of the class and read a book, waiting for Hylton's chauffeur to collect him in his master's limousine. It was a curious adolescence. Separated from his home and family, surrounded by grown-up entertainers, passing through a rapid succession of schools and theatres, it made him seem more sophisticated yet less worldly than his peers. He was a precocious innocent, cast adrift in an adult world.

Ernie wasn't the only child star in Jack Hylton's showbiz stable. Whenever Hylton went on tour, he was always on the look-out for raw talent, and the easiest way of finding it was to audition local juveniles in the venue before the show. Oblivious to the notion that he might easily be replaced as Hylton's favourite, Ernie liked to sit in on these auditions, and when the show reached Manchester he took his usual seat alongside Hylton in the stalls. Ernie had already seen all sorts, even after a few months in the business, but the lad who got up onstage that day was something else. His singing wasn't bad at all but his Bud Flanagan impression was even better. Whoever he was, this Eric Bartholomew was clearly a born entertainer. Ernie was impressed – and also rather worried. 'Bye then, Ernie,' said the boys in the band. 'Things won't be the same with this new lad around, but I dare say we'll soon get used to him. What are you going to do now?'[8]

'Two-ton' Tessie O'Shea (left) who performed many times with Eric and Ernie at Variety theatres up and down the land.

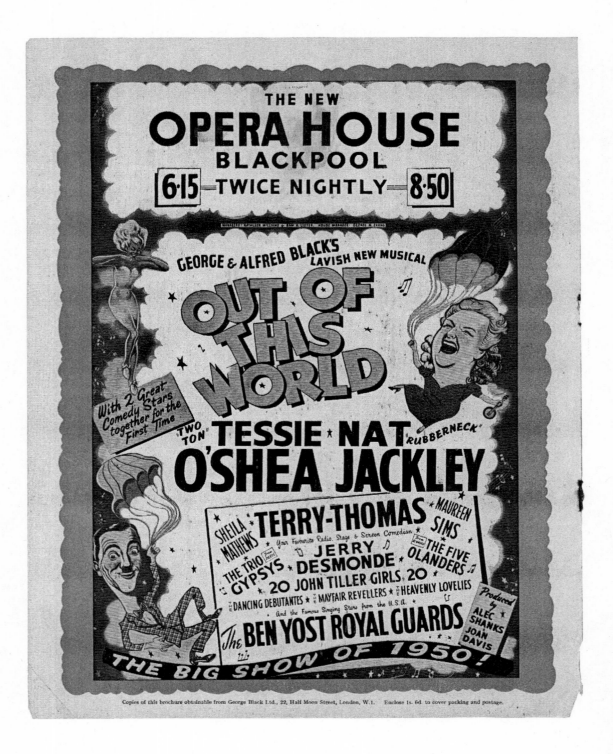

CHAPTER 4

YOUTH TAKES A BOW

BRITAIN'S GREATEST DOUBLE ACT might have got together a little earlier
if it hadn't been for an awkward diplomatic incident commonly known as
World War Two. A few weeks after Eric auditioned for Jack Hylton, Britain
declared war on Germany and fearful of imminent bombardment, His
Majesty's Government ordered all the theatres in the country to close.
George Bernard Shaw wrote an indignant letter to *The Times*, reminding
readers of the morale-building role the theatres had played during the First
World War, and less than a fortnight later they reopened, but by now Hylton's
musicians were being called up for the forces and he had to disband his show.
Hylton returned to Villa Daheim, his family home on the Sussex coast. He
invited Ernie to come with him.

Villa Daheim was even grander than the Shaftesbury Hotel. Ernie had never been abroad, and for this railwayman's son from East Ardsley the Sussex coast seemed like Hawaii. 'I was born poor,' Hylton used to say, 'and now I have it, I'm going to enjoy it.'[1] He made sure Ernie enjoyed it too. Hylton had a cook, a maid, a chauffeur and a nanny, and he treated Ernie like one of the family, giving him free bed and board and five shillings pocket money every week. George Black, who ran the London Palladium, had a house nearby, and his children, George, Alfred and Paula, were frequent visitors to Villa Daheim. Hylton had a wife and two daughters, Jackie and Georgie, and Ernie soon came to feel like his adopted son.

Yet in the midst of all this friendly affluence, Ernie began to feel homesick. He'd been away from home for many months, and in his absence his five-year-old kid brother, Arthur, had died of peritonitis. As the eldest child, Ernie felt a strong sense of duty to his family. He asked Hylton if he could go home. 'Of course,' said Hylton, and bought him a train ticket back to Leeds, but Ernie didn't return home to the warm welcome he deserved. When he arrived, he found his father sitting at the table. 'Why did you come back home?' asked his dad, without a flicker of emotion. 'You had it made.'[2]

What with the outbreak of the Second World War to think about, and all its attendant complications, it was hardly surprising that it took Hylton some time to write to Sadie Bartholomew about her son. Yet eventually, after several months of waiting, the summons finally arrived. Eric was invited to join Bryan Michie's 'discoveries' show, *Youth Takes A Bow*, at £5 a week. Michie's show was touring around the country, and Eric joined the company at the Nottingham Empire. Sadie came with him – he was still only thirteen, after all. Agreeable as ever, her husband George stayed at home in Morecambe, working for the local council, as he always had done. It was lucky for Eric that he had no siblings to compete for his mum's attention. It was lucky for Sadie that her husband was benign enough to let her go.

A fiver a week was a decent wage in 1939 (especially for a boy barely into his teens) but it was a fraction of the three-figure sums that Michie and Hylton were earning, and Eric reckoned he was 'well and truly exploited'.[3] Still, it was a great show in which to learn his trade, and he wound up playing all sorts of parts, far more varied than the impressions he'd done at his audition. In a routine called 'Dancing Through The Ages', he even played a ninety-seven year old codger, in a bald wig. This was a lot more fun than schoolwork, and he was a lot better at it. Like many bright boys who hate to sit in stuffy classrooms, he had a natural aptitude for learning on the job.

The first half of the show was performed by adults, the second half by kids like Eric, and together they represented a veritable academy of Light Entertainment. The star of the second half was a girl called Mary Naylor. She was the same age as Eric, but she made him look like an untried amateur – which, essentially, he still was. Born in Nottingham she'd made her stage debut at the Nottingham Empire, at the tender age of twelve. Still only thirteen when Eric met her, she'd already appeared on Jack Hylton's radio show, and even been seen on a newfangled contraption called television. An actress, a singer and an accomplished musician, she sang an Andrews Sisters number called 'The Ferryboat Serenade', self-accompanied on the accordion.

These songs were terribly tame compared to teenage pop songs today. A girl called Vera Howe sang a song about her favourite dress ('till it wilted I wore it, I'll always adore it, my sweet little Alice Blue Gown') and a lad called Stanley Ambler sang a hymn to lifelong fidelity called 'I'll Walk Beside You' which even the spinsters in the audience might have found a trifle sentimental. However, the glory of Variety was its sheer variety, and it wasn't just singers on this adolescent bill. There was a fourteen-year-old acrobat called Jean Bamforth and a spirited girl called Dorothy Duval who stomped about in a pair of gigantic boots. 'It was quite something to see that little titch leap out from the wings straight into a big walloping routine,'[4] said Eric. There was a young man called Frank Hines who impersonated Charlie Chaplin, with a flickering spotlight that gave his act the appearance of a silent film. Most notably there was Arthur Tolcher, a teenager who played the harmonica and the ukulele – often at the same time. The son of two music-hall artistes, he'd been on the boards since he was eleven. Eric and Ernie never forgot about him, and years later he became a regular on their TV show where, resplendent in white tie and tails, he would raise his mouth organ to his lips, only to be told, 'Not now, Arthur' at the end of every show. 'He did this extraordinary act with the harmonica,' recalls Patrick Newley, a former actor and comedian, now a journalist for *The Stage*, who worked with Arthur at Butlins towards the end of his long career. 'He'd

'I'm not all there' was the first thing Ernie ever saw Eric perform on a stage when young Eric auditioned for Jack Hylton in Manchester. Eric's early performance is captured here in this delightful illustration by Edwin Hall.

play all different types of harmonica. There was a great large one and there was one that was about one inch long. He was incredibly energetic. He used to wear tons of make-up and a dinner jacket. It looked comic but he took it completely seriously. It went down a storm with the audience. They absolutely adored him.'

The grown-up half of the bill was even more lively. There was a dance act, the Danny Lipton Trio, two singing sisters, Rosie and Alice Lloyd, a drunk act called Archie Glen, and 'Two Ton' Tessie O'Shea, a robust Welsh comedienne who once made her grand entrance on an elephant (the elephant didn't much care for lugging two tons of comedienne about – he hurled her off, putting her out of the show for weeks).[5] Like Tessie's elephant, these entertainers had long memories: Rosie and Alice Lloyd were the sisters of Marie Lloyd, the Queen of Edwardian Music Hall, and Archie Glen had served his apprenticeship with Fred Karno, the great impresario who taught Charlie Chaplin and Stan Laurel their trade. Grand Variety theatres like the Nottingham Empire had replaced the intimate music halls of the Victorian era, but Eric had joined an ensemble whose roots stretched right back to that golden age.

After a week in Nottingham, this colourful troupe continued their nationwide tour, and Eric went with them, playing a new town every week, twice nightly, six nights a week, with Sadie at his side. This remorseless slog prompted a constant stream of casualties (especially among boy sopranos, whose voices had a nasty habit of breaking in mid-performance). Since only the most gifted and dedicated juveniles could stay the course, Bryan Michie had to call on a constant supply of adolescent reinforcements. And so, when the company reached Swansea, Eric was reunited with Ernie Wise.

Ernie had spent a difficult few months in Leeds. He'd left home a promising amateur, he'd returned a seasoned pro, and he found it impossible to resume his old double act with his father. 'The magic had vanished forever,'[6] he reflected, sadly. A gap had opened up between them that would never close. Ernie did a few solo turns in the working men's clubs, just to make ends meet. When his dad first took him to these clubs, a few years before, they'd seemed such thrilling places. Now he found all the fun had disappeared. To return to the old haunts he thought he'd left behind became such torture that in the end he jacked it all in and got a job on the local coal round. From appearing on the West End stage for £6 a week, he was now appearing on a horse and cart for seventeen shillings and sixpence, lugging sacks of coal around the streets of Leeds. When a telegram arrived from Bryan Michie, asking him to join *Youth Takes A Bow* in Swansea, on £7 a week, it was a wonderful reprieve.

CHAPTER 5

MORECAMBE & WISE

ERIC AND ERNIE SOON BECAME GOOD PALS, but it was the unremitting grind of touring which turned them into a double act. From week to week, the routine never varied. The working week began and ended on Sunday, when they'd pack their bags and travel on to the next town on their itinerary. They went by steam train — back then, only the biggest stars travelled by car. Every Sunday several thousand entertainers would make the same journey, criss-crossing the country en route to the next town and the next show. Old friends and former colleagues would often meet up at Crewe Station, that trainspot-ter's mecca where every Variety artiste in Britain seemed to be changing trains. However these brief encounters were just about the only source of excite-ment. On the whole, it was a pretty tedious way to spend your one day off a week. Trains were slower then, Sunday trains even more so, and the added disruptions of wartime meant the journey often took all day. No wonder Eric described these cross-country treks as 'marathons of mind-numbing boredom'.[1] Some performers played poker to while away the time. 'We saw men lose entire pay packets on a journey,' said Eric. 'Ernie and I were put off gambling for life.'[2] Being in showbusiness was enough of a gamble in itself.

To relieve the tedium of train travel, Eric became an avid reader. He'd never been a keen student, but now his schooldays were behind him he became increasingly aware that he'd left school at an early age without much of an education, and he became increasingly determined to educate himself, one way or another. Train carriages became his libraries, where he devoured all kinds of books – anything he could get his hands on. It was during these journeys that he discovered Charles Dickens, particularly *The Pickwick Papers*, which remained his favourite book throughout his life, and the funniest thing he'd ever read. During one train journey he was even asked to leave the compartment because he was crying tears of laughter as he read it. You can see why Eric was so fond of Dickens. The picaresque world of Variety, with its sentimentality and cruelty and its flamboyant but brittle characters was one Dickens would have recognized immediately, and whose Victorian forebears he had described.

When they finally arrived they'd tramp the streets, looking for a room in a cheap (and hopefully cheerful) guest house – only really big stars could afford to stay in proper hotels. These rooms could be cosy, but they were never glamorous. 'A pot of aspidistras,' said Eric, describing the typical bed-and-breakfast décor, 'a "Stag At Bay" on one wall, a flight of china ducks on another, a roaring coal fire, and a gasunda, a pot that goes under the bed.'[3]

Normally it wasn't too hard to find a room, though the quality varied wildly. Some of the better boarding houses wouldn't put up 'theatricals'. Some even discriminated between 'legitimate' and 'illegitimate' entertainers, between (relatively) respectable actors and disreputable Variety artistes. A landlady wouldn't need to see you perform to know what sort of act you were, only where you were playing. The Birmingham Hippodrome was one of Eric's favourite Variety theatres, but some of the local B&Bs would only put up artistes who played the Theatre Royal, which staged straight plays.

In spite of this petty snobbery (or perhaps because of it) Variety artistes had more fun. One of Eric and Ernie's favourite guest houses was Mrs McKay's at 11 Daisy Avenue, Manchester, which consisted of two adjoining buildings –

The only known photograph showing Eric and Ernie as part of a trio before they settled on a winning formula. Who is the mystery woman? Answers on a postcard!

one for actors, the other for Variety artistes. They were laughing and joking in their room one night when they heard Dame Flora Robson calling across the great divide. 'It's so dull over here,' boomed the Great British Actress. 'Can I join in?' Twenty years later, the boys returned the compliment, by inviting her on to their TV show. She was glad to take part. 'People often think I'm dead,' she said, 'and that can sometimes lose me quite a lot of work.'[4]

Mrs McKay was quite a character in her own right. She was renowned for her malapropisms. 'I've had muriels painted on the bathroom walls,' she used to say, 'and pelvises fitted all along the tops of the windows.'[5] She used to listen out for double footsteps on the landing, a surefire sign that one of her guests was smuggling a girlfriend up to bed. One night, her suspicion was aroused by the sound of unusually heavy footsteps, and she raced on to the landing to find a comedian carrying a girl upstairs on his back. Eric used Mrs McKay as the basis for a character called Annie (with a fondness for similar malapropisms) in his second novel, *Stella*, finished by Eric's son Gary after Eric died.

Other landladies were more concerned about the quality of their guests' acts. The boys knew an old comedian called Bill Burke, who'd 'died' in Morecambe on a Monday, the night when local landladies went to see the show for free. He returned to his lodgings to lick his wounds and eat his dinner, only to discover that his landlady had been along to see the show. 'There's no supper for you tonight,' she told him. 'You were bloody awful.'[6] Eric and Ernie's old friend Harry Secombe went one better. 'You're not staying in my house,' said his landlady, after his celebrated shaving routine got the slow handclap in Bolton. 'You can get the first train in the morning.'

Most landladies were far more friendly, even if the service was hardly five star. Welsh comic Wyn Calvin once returned to his boarding house after a show at the Swansea Empire and decided to take a bath before his supper. However as he lay in the hot soapy tub, he heard a voice outside the bathroom door. 'Mr Calvin!' called out the landlady. 'Are you in the bath?' 'Yes,' replied Wyn, wearily. 'Well, be careful,' she said, 'I just painted it.'

Jokes about bad guest houses were the product of painful experience, like the one about the landlady who asks a guest if he has a good memory for faces. 'Why?' he asks. 'Because there's no shaving mirror in the bathroom,' she replies. Legend has it that the comedian Frank Randle started a small fire in a hotel whose service had displeased him, but most entertainers made do with

leaving that cryptic (but damning) warning in the visitor's book, 'I shall certainly tell my friends.' Eric and Ernie used to tell a joke about a double act who book into a boarding house with a bottle of sherry, which they leave on the dining-room sideboard. They decide not to drink any of it until the end of the week, and so they're furious when they find the bottle is a little emptier every day. Assuming their landlady has been helping herself, they take their revenge on her by pissing in it, and when they say goodbye at the end of the week, they're both feeling rather smug. Sure enough, the landlady apologizes for helping herself to their tipple. 'But you like your trifle so much,' she adds, 'that I knew you wouldn't mind me putting a drop of your sherry in it every night.'

*   *   *

Most of the time, Eric and Ernie had no trouble finding lodgings. However, on the night the company arrived in Oxford to play the New Theatre (still there today, unlike a lot of Variety theatres), the town was full of troops and rooms of any sort were in short supply. Sadie eventually found a place for her and Eric, but Ernie had no grown-up to help him (he was still only fifteen) and at ten o'clock at night he was still traipsing the streets, looking for somewhere to stay. Luckily he was rescued by a teenage singer called Doreen Stephens, who took him round to Sadie's. 'He can come in with us,' Sadie told her. 'I'll sleep in the single bed and the two boys can share the double.'[7] From then on they shared a double bed and Sadie looked after both of them. The bed they shared on TV harked back to those early days. At first they did it to save money, but Sadie ended up treating Ernie as her son. By the time they could afford separate beds again, they'd become the best of friends.

The shortage of wartime accommodation also brought Eric and Ernie together onstage. They were playing Birmingham, with a week in Coventry to follow, when Coventry was blitzed by the Luftwaffe. The theatre had survived but the digs they'd booked were flattened, so they stayed on in Birmingham and commuted to Coventry every day. It was only twenty miles but the Blitz was causing chaos and the train went at a crawl. The boys soon became restless, so

Sadie suggested they work up a double act to pass the time. She even bought them a tape recorder, to help them polish the routine. They pinched a string of gags from older entertainers, and one of their co-stars, Alice Lloyd, suggested a song for them to finish on, with a soft shoe shuffle – 'By The Light of The Silvery Moon'. Even though Alice was the sister of Marie Lloyd, the Queen of Music Hall, show business has never made any allowances for repu-tations. When *Youth Takes A Bow* reached Liverpool, Jack Hylton came to see the show, and the boys did their double act for him in the interval. 'The act's not bad,' he told them, 'but don't sing that bloody song.'[8] Sadie had another word with Alice, Alice suggested 'Only A Bird In A Gilded Cage', and at the Liverpool Empire in 1941, Morecambe & Wise made their debut.

Except they weren't called Morecambe & Wise. Eric was still plain old Eric Bartholomew, but no one really liked the sound of Bartholomew & Wise. The problem was solved by Adelaide Hall, a black singer from Brooklyn. She'd worked with Duke Ellington at the Cotton Club prior to touring with *Youth Takes A Bow* so Sadie thought she might be able to conjure up a decent stage name. 'There's this friend of mine, a coloured boy who calls himself Rochester because he comes from Rochester, Minnesota,' said her husband, Bert Hicks. 'Where do you come from?'[9]

'Morecambe,' she replied.

CHAPTER 6

THE GLASGOW EMPIRE

JACK HYLTON WATCHED ERIC AND ERNIE from the wings of the Liverpool
Empire. He was so impressed, he told Bryan Michie to let them do their double
act every night the following week. Trouble was, their next stop was the
dreaded Glasgow Empire – the graveyard of English comedians. Singers usually
went down pretty well, but Sassenach comics were guaranteed a rocky ride.
Ken Dodd called this place the House of Terror, Des O'Connor fainted onstage
in mid-routine, and even Max Miller, a massive star down south, didn't relish
playing there. 'I'm a comedian, not a missionary,' he used to say.

Max was a wise man. These hecklers could be ruthless. 'If they like you,'
people used to say, 'they let you live.' When Mike and Bernie Winters played

Above **The torture chamber for Southern artistes performing in the city. Eric and Ernie recalled walking both on
and off the stage to the sound of their own footfalls.**

there, Mike came on first, followed by Bernie. 'Jesus Christ, there's two of them!'[1] shouted a joker in the stalls – and that was one of the nicer heckles, as the amiable English comic Jimmy Edwards discovered, to his cost. 'Why don't you just fuck off?' suggested a heckler, during Jimmy's act. 'I beg your pardon?' replied Jimmy, lamely, far too shocked to summon up a more amusing riposte. 'You heard what my friend said,' replied another punter. 'Why don't you just fuck off?'[2] Debonair English duo George and Kenneth Western once ended up in hospital after a nasty car crash. When Kenneth finally came round, George asked him how he felt. 'Bloody dreadful,' replied Kenneth, 'but not so bad as I did at the Glasgow Empire.'[3]

Despite its ferocious reputation, the Glasgow Empire wasn't a dump. On the contrary, it was spotless, with marble staircases, sparkling chandeliers and golden cherubs around the walls. 'It was a beautifully run theatre,' said Ernie, 'but you felt you were a foreigner. Nobody spoke to you and the audiences were hard – hard to please.'[4] Welsh comic Wyn Calvin used to play up his accent, to make sure the audience didn't think he was English. 'Everybody gets the bird on Friday night,' the theatre manager used to warn outsiders, 'and remember, no football gags on Saturday night.'[5]

For a lot of 'foreign' comics, the language barrier was another problem. With its dependence on rhythm and wordplay, humour is especially resistant to translation, even from one dialect to another. One unfamiliar word can squash a punchline or kill a laugh. Yet Eric and Ernie's act consisted of such awful groaners – the sort of corny puns that wouldn't look out of place inside a Christmas cracker – that their material was immune to such subtleties. Their gags were dreadful but that hardly mattered. It was their personalities that counted, and Eric and Ernie were almost impossible to dislike, even if these punters did their best not to show it. 'They're beginning to like you,' said the stage manager, as they walked off to the sound of their own footsteps.

As it turned out, their biggest problem wasn't the audience but one of the other acts. Some of Eric and Ernie's worst gags were of their own invention, but most of their better ones were 'borrowed' from older comics. One of their hardy perennials – 'I have enough money to last me for the rest of my life, if I drop dead at six o'clock tonight' – was half-inched from Dickie Hassett, a Cockney stand-up who appeared in *Youth Takes A Bow*. Pinching material was far more common then than it is today, but it still didn't pay to be caught red-handed. In Glasgow they were confronted in the wings by an indignant stand-up called Scott Saunders who accused them of using one of his old one-liners. Eric and Ernie swore blind that they'd stolen it from someone else. Begrudgingly, Saunders agreed to let them use it that week. Yet when they cracked the same joke the next night ('my wife was sent to me from heaven – as a punishment') it was greeted with an awkward silence. The same thing happened the next night, and the next. Only at the end of the week did they discover that Saunders had started using the same joke in the first half, killing this gag, and undercutting the remainder of their fledgling act.

Despite this hiccup Eric and Ernie went down fairly well in Glasgow, but they still struggled to get a regular slot for their double act. This had nothing to do with the quality of their material (or the lack of it) and everything to do with the office politics of *Youth Takes A Bow*. Making space for their double act meant dropping one of the other juveniles, and since most of these little darlings were accompanied by their mothers, Michie knew whoever he left out would give him hell. As a former music-hall performer, Arthur Tolcher's mum was an especially tricky prospect. She used to sit in the wings on an old wardrobe basket. She was always knitting, but she never missed a thing.

Yet as the war dragged on, Michie's prodigies began to drift away. Eventually the only juveniles left were Jean Bamforth, the teenage acrobat, and Eric and Ernie. Ernie would start the show, singing 'Run Rabbit Run', Eric would follow him singing 'I'm Not All There', Jean would do some acrobatics, Eric and Ernie would do their double act, and then the three of them would finish on an old blues number, 'The Waiter, The Porter and The Upstairs Maid'. By now Michie was sufficiently impressed (or desperate) to buy them matching blue blazers and straw boaters. It was the first time they'd dressed alike onstage, and it made a big difference. Back then, most double acts consisted of a comic and a straight man. Eric had started out as a clown. Ernie started out as his feed. Dressing identically encouraged them to blur these boundaries. Ernie was still the straight man, but he became more playful. Eric was still the comic, but he started cracking wisecracks, rather than simply playing the fool.

However, they didn't have much time to hone their act, since by now the Blitz was beginning to bite. Resourceful as ever, they made a bit of extra

In addition to worrying where they would be appearing on the poster, as relative unknowns Eric and Ernie also had to contend with promoters who couldn't even be bothered to bill them correctly.

money firewatching – sitting up all night playing cards in empty theatres, keeping a lookout for any incendiary bombs that might set the roof alight. It was supposed to be a grown-up job, but the adults in the cast were happy to pay Eric and Ernie half a crown to do it for them. Ernie banked his half-crown. Eric spent his on cigarettes, which he chainsmoked throughout the night. Luckily every night they spent firewatching passed off without incident, but other theatres weren't so lucky. The legendary Jimmy James was playing the Crown Theatre in Eccles when a bomb shattered the windows and blew down all the doors. 'It's that wedding party at the back again,' observed Jimmy, nonchalantly. 'Will someone tell them either to shut up or get out?'[6] As Eric told Jimmy's son, many years later, Eric and Ernie often used his dad's material – partly as a tribute to a great comic, but mainly because it was so funny.

By the time they reached the Sheffield Empire the Blitz had become so fierce that performances were switched to two o'clock and five-thirty, so punters and performers could disperse before the blackout. It was a novelty to have the evening off, but they weren't really able to enjoy it. There was a big hole in their bedroom wall – the result of a previous air-raid – and although they were frozen stiff they were far too shy to ask their formidable landlady for an extra blanket. 'If an air-raid warning be received during the performance the audience will be informed,' read the programme, demurely. 'Those desiring to leave the theatre may do so, but the performance will continue.' Most punters stuck it out, and so did Eric and Ernie. They soldiered on until 1942 when Michie closed the show, leaving them out of work.

Eric returned to Morecambe and a job at the local razorblade factory. Ernie returned to Leeds and his old job on the local coal round. Eric hated making razorblades but he was easygoing, like his dad, and he might never have got back into showbiz if Ernie hadn't fled to Morecambe. Three months lugging sacks of coal was all that Ernie could endure. Surely there must be a way to revive their fledgling double act? They returned to London and Sadie went with them. They found a flat in Mornington Crescent, not far from Euston Station, and went along to the London Hippodrome to audition for a new show called *Strike A New Note*. When they arrived, they found the show's producer in the stalls. It was George Black, Jack Hylton's old neighbour from Angmering-on-Sea. Sitting alongside him were his sons, Alfred and George Junior, and his pretty daughter, Paula. Ernie knew them all from his happy days at Hylton's seaside villa. Heartened by the sight of a few familiar faces, Eric and Ernie performed their whole act, which now lasted an entire nine minutes, and Black offered to take them both on at £10 each a week.

During the early days, Eric and Ernie had to travel to wherever the bookings were. Top left **Eric** enjoys a stick of rock backstage at the Leeds Empire. Left **Ernie** observes the local fishing boats at Ramsgate. Above a poster shows how, even in 1950, they were top of the bill.

Below By contrast, this photograph of the cast at the Empire Swansea, 1948–9, shows them not quite important enough to avoid being obscured by the other performers in the panto!

Above and right **Eric and Doreen taken by her future husband, Ernie.**

Below **Eric looks like he's up to mischief. The boy with the big tie is Stan Stennett's eldest son, Roger.**

CHAPTER 7

STRIKE A NEW NOTE

THE PRINCE OF WALES was a brand new 'tits and feathers' theatre, custom-built for Variety shows. Even today its striking art deco design still looks daring and futuristic, but back then architecture was the last thing on Eric and Ernie's minds. 'These boys and girls have been gathered from every part of the country,' read the sign outside the theatre. 'All are players of experience, needing but the opportunity to make themselves known. They have worked, they have learned. This, then, is their chance to show what they are worth.' Eric and Ernie could hardly have put it better themselves. They hadn't been hired to do their double act, just bits and pieces, but it was great to be back in showbiz, and *Strike A New Note* was a big hit. It ran for over a year.

Ernie kept a copy of the original programme, and today it makes fascinating reading, though you need pretty good eyesight to spot his name (and

Above **Theatre impresario George Black.**

Eric's) among the 'wines and spirits' at the bottom of the bill. Eric was such small fry that they couldn't even be bothered to spell his surname correctly. Not for the first time (nor the last) he was billed as Eric Morecombe. Clearly, his home-town wasn't quite so well known down south. It's an exquisite irony, since today he's by far the most famous name in this list of unfamiliar hopefuls, and it makes this programme seem even more precious, like a mis-printed Penny Black. 'Here is youth,' declared the blurb, but the show's star, Sid Field, was hardly youthful. He was almost forty when the show began, and his straight man, Jerry Desmonde, was already in his mid-thirties. However this Brummie comic and his feed were virtually unknown in London, and so George Black billed them as 'The Rising Generation'. Black had spotted them in pantomime in Nottingham, but Eric and Ernie already knew all about them. They'd been one of their earliest influences, ever since *Youth Takes A Bow*.

While the rest of London sat back and laughed, Eric and Ernie looked on and learned. In Field's daft sketches you can trace the origins of much of Eric and Ernie's TV humour, as Field played a golfer, a snooker player, a musician, a photographer and a spiv called Slasher Green. 'It's not so much what I say that's funny, it's the way I say it,'[1] Field used to say. That late great straight man, Len Lowe, put it even better. 'A comedian says funny things,' he said. 'A great comedian says things funny.'[2] You could say the same thing about Eric and Ernie (sitting in Eric's study, leafing through their handwritten joke books, long after they'd both died, I realized I'd read better gags on the end of lollipop sticks, but when I heard them it was another matter).

They learnt another lesson too. Watching entertainers losing their pay packets playing poker had put them right off gambling, and Sid Field's fondness for liquid refreshment was a graphic illustration of the dangers of strong drink. *Strike A New Note* made Field a star, but he didn't have long to enjoy it. Sadly, this lovely man was dead before the decade was out – his demise hastened by demon drink.

Field's premature death left Desmonde high and dry. His posh stage persona fell out of fashion. Although he lived until 1967, he ended up driving a cab. Most double acts crashed and burned, one way or another, and Eric and Ernie saw enough of these ruined relationships at close quarters to instill in them a steely determination not to end up the same way.

* * *

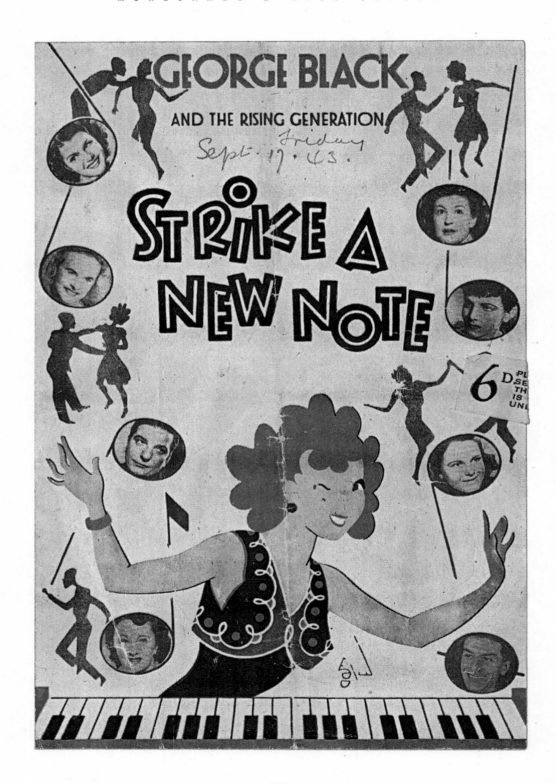

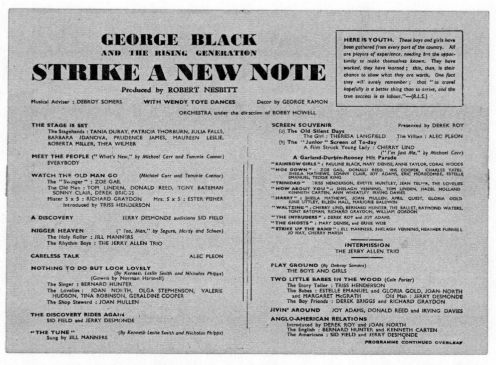

Opposite and above *Strike a New Note* was a huge West End success in 1943. Eric and Ernie were only playing bit-parts, but it looked mighty good on their CVs.

Field and Desmonde weren't the only decent comics in *Strike A New Note*. Derek Roy, aka The Fun Doctor, was another rising star (after the war he became a radio star on *Variety Bandbox* alongside Frankie Howerd) and the 'second-string' comic was Alec Pleon, aka Mr Funny Face ('funny face they call me – funny face, that's me'). Like Arthur Tolcher, his mum and dad had done a double act in the halls, and his gurning and yodelling owed a lot to old-time Music Hall. However, since George Black had promised Eric and Ernie they could do their double act if Pleon was ever indisposed, they took a rather more morbid interest in him. 'Eric and I prayed every day that Alec Pleon would fall ill, or take the wrong bus, or be arrested,' said Ernie, 'but he turned out to be the fittest man in showbusiness.'[3] Eventually, Pleon did miss a couple of shows, and Eric and Ernie got their big break, but it merely confirmed that Black was quite right to confine them to bit parts. 'The audience simply stared at us, open-mouthed, aghast, wondering what was being inflicted on them, and why.'[4] They'd already learnt an awful lot, but they still had much more to learn.

Star of *Strike A New Note* Sid Field. The comedian is pictured here with a young Petula Clark in a publicity still from *London Town* in 1946.

Yet whatever they lacked in stagecraft, they made up for in self-confidence. Because of the Blitz and the blackout, performances of *Strike A New Note* were 'twice daily' rather than 'twice nightly', leaving them free to moonlight in the evenings. By now America had joined the war and Mary Naylor, their old pal from *Youth Takes A Bow*, was playing the US Officers' Club in Knightsbridge. Eric and Ernie tagged along, did their double act, and were rewarded with American ice cream, chewing gum and Chesterfield cigarettes – scarce and precious in ration-book Britain.

The Second World War was a mixed blessing for Variety. Seaside resorts like Morecambe struggled, but after a slow start the West End boomed. Aircraft and munitions factories guaranteed full employment, and with luxury goods and even clothing rationed, there wasn't much else to spend your wages on. Since domestic coal was rationed, why stay at home and freeze? For blitzed-out civilians on the home front as well as soldiers on leave, the knowledge that tonight might be your last encouraged folk to let their hair down. Better to all die together in a crowded theatre than on your own at home. People had enough doom and gloom in their daily lives without going to see something heavy. They wanted cheering up and shared laughter is a wonderful cure-all. With its Judy Garland numbers and minstrel songs like 'Nigger Heaven' (deeply patronizing, but not an outright insult back then), no wonder *Strike A New Note* did such brisk trade.

Yet although it was a feelgood show, it still revealed quite a lot about the preoccupations of those times. Pleon's monologue was called 'Careless Talk' (as in the wartime poster, 'careless talk costs lives'), Field and Desmonde were improbably cast as a couple of Yanks in a sketch called 'Anglo-American Relations', and Ernie impersonated James Cagney singing the title song from Cagney's Academy Award-winning movie, *Yankee Doodle Dandy*. One night Hollywood star Adolphe Menjou (most famous for his Oscar-nominated role in *The Front Page*) came backstage and congratulated Ernie in person – quite an accolade, considering he wasn't even one of the principals. At least Ernie could console himself that someone had spotted his star quality. Eric had to make do with a place in the chorus line.

They grew up fast. Their cramped dressing-room (which they shared with another future star, the indefatigable all-rounder Billy Dainty) overlooked the Mapleton Hotel, where American GIs used to go for an 'afternoon shack-up' (as Eric put it) and the girls in the chorus line weren't remotely bothered about Eric or Ernie seeing them in the buff. Actually, this wasn't so much of

Sid Field's partner and straight-man, Jerry Desmonde, seen here in the 1960s show, *Hit The Limit*.

The Queen of Hearts, Newcastle Empire, with Sheila Mathews as Jocelyn, 'a wandering minstrel'.

a compliment as a subtle put-down, but Eric and Ernie were oblivious to any slight. They were too busy enjoying the view.

Anyone who was anyone came to see *Strike A New Note*, even The Man Who Never Was. This was the nickname of a dead body dumped in the Med by a British submarine, dressed up as a Royal Marines officer, carrying top-secret plans for an invasion of Sardinia (the real invasion was planned for Sicily). To fool the Germans, all sorts of items were planted in his pockets, including love letters, unpaid bills, and two tickets for *Strike A New Note*.

Living visitors to the show included Clark Gable, Alfred Hitchcock, George Raft and James Stewart, and Eric and Ernie were invited to parties at swish nightclubs like the Bagatelle. Not bad going for a couple of northern lads who were still only sixteen and seventeen. It got better. When Sid Field declined a request to appear in his own radio series, the BBC asked Eric and Ernie to take his place, in a show called *Youth Must Have Its Fling* (since Field was nearly forty, it was just as well he turned it down). Radio was big news in those days, and the broadcast made the local paper back home in Morecambe, in a report that confirmed their double act was already slipping off the traditional straitjacket of comic and feed. 'Ernie was supposed to do the "feeding",' read the review, 'but Eric complained that he took the laughs.'[5]

CHAPTER 8

SHEILA MATHEWS

ONE OF THE CHILD STARS in *Strike A New Note*, alongside Eric and Ernie, was Sheila Mathews, and it was wonderful to find her alive and well, living in a pretty bungalow on the south coast with a lovely view across the Channel. Striking and vivacious, with the charm of a woman half her age, it's hard to believe she's been in the business (initially as a Variety artiste, and subsequently as a successful straight actress) for over seventy years.

Sheila was born in 1927 (a year after Eric, two years after Ernie) and grew up in Muswell Hill, in north London. Her father was a bank clerk. Her mother was a housewife. She started dancing lessons when she was a toddler, and her teacher soon discovered she could sing too. She sang her first solo when she was three. 'My mother should have been on the stage,' says Sheila. 'Of course it wasn't considered the thing to do in those days.' Like Eric's mum

The programme for the 1944 hit show, *Happy & Glorious*, in which seventeen-year-old Sheila appeared alongside the veteran entertainer, Tommy Trinder.

and Ernie's dad, Sheila's mum did her best for her gifted child. 'She loved the theatre and went to see everything, so she used to tell me how to do my numbers. We'd rehearse in the kitchen.' When she was twelve, a kindly couple heard her singing in a concert, and phoned her mother. 'We'd like to teach Sheila singing,' they said. 'We can't afford singing and dancing,' said Sheila's mum. 'We don't want any money,' they said. 'We'll teach her for nothing.' Thanks to their kindness, she was still singing for her supper sixty-two years later, in the West End eight times a week in *Me And My Girl*.

When war broke out, Sheila was evacuated. 'I had to break off all my dancing and my singing lessons,' she says. 'I was so homesick, I cried for two years.' She missed her family dreadfully. She worried about them too. 'All my pocket money was going on phoning home to see if they were all right,' she says. 'It was such an awful time. I didn't know whether mummy and daddy were alive, or if the house was still there.' After two years, she could bear no more. 'I've got to come home,' she told her mum. 'I must go onstage.' The

Above **Sheila**, in top hat and tails, as she appeared in *Happy & Glorious*.

Inset **This** photograph from a concert at Alexandra Palace in 1932 shows that, even at the age of five, Sheila was already a natural entertainer.

Blitz was still in full swing, but her mother took her back to London.

Sheila never went back to school. Instead she learnt to tap-dance with the legendary Buddy Bradley. Born in Pennsylvania in 1908, Bradley was one of New York's finest choreographers in the 1920s and 1930s. He worked with stars like Fred Astaire, but although everyone in the business knew all about him, his work was never publicly acknowledged, because he was black. 'I had

Anne

Sheila Mathews

gay and vivacious ingenue, got her first big chance in George Black's "Strike A New Note" at the Prince of Wales Theatre, London. Since then, she has understudied for Zoe Gail in "Happy And Glorious," appeared successfully in several revues and last winter appeared as Principal Girl in "Dick Whittingdon" at the Manchester Palace.

In this pantomime she had the unusual experience of playing both Principal Girl and Principal Boy. When Jeanne Adrian, who played Dick, was taken ill, Sheila took over for her so successfully that she will again play a Principal Boy rôle this winter.

Sheila says that her most thrilling war-time memory was on D-Day when she was specially selected to sing for the troops just before they embarked for the invasion.

Pamela

A page from the programme of the 1949 show *Midsummer Madness*, at The New Opera House, Blackpool, in which Sheila Mathews appeared.

to audition for him, to see if he would take me, because all the stars used to go and have classes with him every day.' Buddy could tell she had talent. He agreed to take her on. Every day she travelled to his dance studio in Dean Street, Soho, where she danced from 10 a.m. to 4 p.m. Years later, at an audition, a director asked her if she could dance. Suddenly, a familiar voice boomed through the theatre. 'She was the finest tap-dancer I've ever had! She was my star pupil!' It was Buddy. He died in New York, where he'd done so much great work, so much of it unacknowledged, in 1972.

Sheila made her professional debut in *Babes In The Wood* at Edinburgh's King's Theatre. 'It was a dreadful journey up there. I shall never forget it. It took forever. The trains were crowded with troops, and you couldn't see because there was only one blue light bulb because of the blackout. Nobody knew where we were because all the signs were taken down in the stations.' She was still only fourteen. Pantomimes were much more lavish in those days, and despite the war this show was still an extravagant affair, made even more magical by the ration-book austerity outside. 'A full orchestra, a full dancing chorus, showgirls, a singing chorus – you've never seen anything like it. Talk about a stageful!' The scenery was spectacular, too. 'There was a lovely big staircase that we were all supposed to walk down. There was a gap between the steps and I disappeared between them.' These stairs (and the gaps between them) were a familiar feature of stage sets in those days. A generation later, Eric and Ernie recreated the same sequence (complete with the gap between the stairs) with Glenda Jackson on their TV show.

The stars of Sheila's first professional pantomime were Jimmy Jewel and Ben Warriss – one of Britain's leading double acts during the 1940s, and a big influence on Eric and Ernie. Some of their knockabout routines were pure Morecambe & Wise. They even did a sketch about an incompetent classical pianist, in much the same vein as Eric and Ernie's televisual tour de force with André Previn. It was Ben Warriss who told Ernie not to worry about being a straight man. 'It doesn't matter who gets the laughs as long as you get half the money,'[1] he said. Or who gets the girls, he might have added. 'I had such a crush on Jimmy Jewel!' says Sheila. 'I thought he was wonderful!'

After touring in a show called *More New Faces* (produced by Ernie's old friend, Jack Hylton) Sheila made her West End debut in another panto – *Jack and Jill* at His Majesty's Theatre. She only had one line (she can still remem-

Left **Sheila in the title role in** *Dick Whittington*, **Newcastle Empire.**

Opposite **Sheila Mathews playing a spoilt Hollywood starlet in Bolton's Revue, St James' Theatre.**

Overleaf **Sheila and friends provide a spot of glamour in** *Midsummer Madness*, **The New Opera House, Blackpool.**

ber it today) but it was a chance to work with two of the top comics in the country, Arthur Askey and 'Monsewer' Eddie Gray. The principal boy was Florence Desmond, Britain's greatest female impressionist, and the Dame was Bryan Michie, who gave Eric and Ernie their first big break in *Youth Takes A Bow*. While Sheila was in this show she heard about a new revue called *Strike A New Note* at the Prince of Wales Theatre. She auditioned, and ended up in the chorus line, alongside Eric and Ernie, supporting Sid Field.

Sid Field was the greatest comic that Sheila had ever seen. Every night, after she'd done her spot, she'd get changed double-quick and race downstairs to watch him from the wings. So did Eric and Ernie. 'Seeing them on television, I see Sid Field in them so often, because they use the camera like Sid Field used an audience.' That was what Eric and Ernie learnt from Field, the ability to make a bunch of strangers feel like a group of friends. 'Sid Field had wonderful warmth,' says Sheila. 'He had this ability to get the audience on his side.' It's surely no coincidence that these two statements also sum up the appeal of Morecambe & Wise. 'Funnily enough, the first time I really noticed them was when we were watching Sid Field do a sketch called "The Tubular Bells". They were hysterical with laughter, and so were we all. They were always laughing and joking, and longing to get on and do their act.'

Her main memory of Eric is him sitting at the side of the stage, surrounded by the ballet girls. 'He made them all laugh so much. He was so funny.' Eric was her dancing partner. 'He learnt very quickly. They partnered us up because we were both the same height.' They had to do a hoedown

Bolton's Revue, Bolton's Theatre, London, Sheila Mathews (centre) with Reg Varney (right) and Donald Reed (left).

together. This was where Eric and Ernie's song-and-dance numbers on TV started off. 'He used to make me laugh so much. He's the only one that made me wet my knickers onstage!' But Eric didn't just joke around. He was also a super dancer. In fact, Sheila reckons he was even better than Ernie.

It was a thrill to see the Hollywood stars in the audience, over here to help the war effort. 'One girl fell in the orchestra pit when she saw Clark Gable in the front row.' But Sheila was always more thrilled to see Sid Field. 'I shall never forget standing at the side of the stage, having just come off from the opening, and Charlie Henry, who was George Black's right-hand man, had to push Sid on the stage, he was so frightened – he was so scared, he would never have gone on.' Maybe that was why he drank.

But Sheila was less than half Sid's age, and so she knew no such fears. And even the war wasn't quite so scary, now that she was home. 'I remember going to the Palladium one day,' says Sheila. 'I'd saved up all my coupons to get a new winter coat. It was pouring with rain and one of these doodlebugs came over and cut out just above the Palladium.' 'Quick! Get down, Sheila!' said her friend. 'I'm not going to!' said Sheila. 'Not in my new coat!'

CHAPTER 9

LORD JOHN SANGER'S
CIRCUS AND VARIETY

AT LAST IT SEEMED that Eric and Ernie's double act might be about to become established, but in November 1943, just a few months after their first radio series ended, Ernie turned eighteen and was called up. He was given a choice between the army, the merchant navy and the mines. The merchant navy paid the most so, sensible as ever, he opted for that. He was sent to Newcastle to train as a steward, on a liner moored on the Tyne. 'I was trained to wait on tables, trained to set tables, trained to clear tables, trained to lift them, shift them, stack them,'[1] he recalled, ruefully. It was a bit more down to earth than flying Spitfires, but after

Above **When Eric and Ernie became a circus act... Lord John Sanger's tent for his touring show. Sometimes the boys would do their act for as many as ten people! Eric hated it, particularly the indignity of being in full evening dress and Wellington boots to sell tickets at the door.**

his training as a floating waiter, he hoped he might wangle an ocean voyage to America or Australia. Fat chance. Instead he became a steward for the Gas Light and Coke Company, on a ship called *The Firelighter*, whose job was to ferry coal from Tyneside to London. Ernie was the cook. It was the one thing he hadn't been trained to do.

Ernie couldn't cook to save his life, but his fellow seamen didn't seem to care. After all, they had more pressing matters than haute cuisine to occupy their minds. Ferrying coal along the North Sea coast wasn't remotely glamorous, but that didn't stop it being bloody dangerous. Their route was nicknamed E-Boat Alley, on account of the enemy torpedo boats that roamed these waters. However, the closest Ernie came to the hereafter was entirely at his own hand. He was transferred to a tanker, delivering aviation fuel to Southampton, and no naked flame was allowed onboard during loading or unloading, for fear that a stray spark might ignite their explosive cargo. Oblivious to this strict safety rule, Ernie used a blowtorch to heat up the soup. Luckily, he avoided blowing the entire ship's company to kingdom come.

The bright side was that between voyages Ernie was ashore for as much as six weeks at a time, and he used this shore leave to rekindle his Variety career. He got back in touch with Jack Hylton's old sidekick, Bryan Michie, who was touring yet another 'discoveries' show around the country. Ernie was a bit too old to be a child prodigy (he was all of eighteen by now) so Michie milked his wartime service for all it was worth. Ernie performed in full naval uniform, billed as 'a boy from the brave Merchant Navy'. By the time he was de-mobbed, he'd pretty much forgotten all about being in a double act with anyone. For the time being, he felt far happier on his own.

*   *   *

Eric and Ernie with Ernie's future wife, Doreen (second right) and friend.

Since Eric was younger than Ernie, he wasn't called up for another six months, and his loyalty to Ernie didn't extend to enlisting in the merchant navy. He stayed on in *Strike A New Note* until it closed, and then became the feed for Gus Morris, a kindly comic from Blackpool who'd won the Military Medal (and lost an eye) during the First World War. Gus had been crippled by machine-gun fire – he couldn't bend his knees – and Eric was a bespectacled (and somewhat sickly-looking) lad of seventeen. They must have made a touching but poignant picture as they traipsed around the halls. After a week in St Helens they had a week off, so Eric went back to Morecambe, but by now he'd turned eighteen, and his home leave was rudely interrupted when he was sent down the mines. The letter arrived on Monday. He was told to start on Wednesday. Gus Morris would have to find himself another straight man. Eric ended up in Accrington, working in a mine that had been condemned twenty years before. He found lodgings with a former miner ('his face tattooed blue with coal dust under the skin, his lungs brittle with silicosis')[2], who woke him up at half past five every morning with a fried breakfast. It was arduous and dangerous work (some of the seams were only two feet high) and Eric lasted less than a year before he was invalided out with heart trouble, and a lifelong aversion to the smell of eggs and bacon. Up until this point he'd only ever been sickly-looking. From now on he ws genuinely sickly, and he would be plagued by ill-health, on and off, until the day he died. Exempt from further service, Eric spent six months as the feed for a comedian called Billy Revel, and after that he got another job, this time with Lord John Sanger's travelling circus. Again, for the third time running, Eric was hired as the straight man. Would he ever get to play the funny man again? To add insult to his injured pride, Sanger's comic wasn't a grizzled veteran, like Gus Morris, but a lad his own age – a recently demobbed ship steward. Imagine Eric's surprise when he discovered that this 'boy from the brave Merchant Navy' was none other than Ernie Wise.

Reunited as a double act, their roles temporarily reversed, Eric and Ernie set out on tour in an old RAF trailer, which they shared with a pipe-smoking pianist called Anton Petrov. Ernie was on £12 a week but Eric had to make do with a tenner, and it wasn't all that long before their pay was cut in half. The reason for this pay cut was the singular unpopularity of Lord John Sanger's Circus and Variety, which turned out to be a showbiz misadventure of almost Pythonesque proportions. As the name suggested, the idea was to combine Circus and Variety acts in a big-top show, which would travel to towns too small to have their own theatre. 'In principle, I suppose, it should have been

quite a promising innovation,' reflected Ernie. 'In practice, though, it turned out to be the lowest common denominator of both.'[3]

To be fair, not all the acts were all that bad. A chap called Walter Lucken did a nice line in performing dogs and horses, and one of the singers, a girl called Molly Seddon ('a thrill to your eyes, ears and heart') had even been on the BBC. Yet the threadbare nature of Lord Sanger's show was encapsulated by the resident clown, 'Speedy' Yelding, who doubled up as a trapeze artiste — and a cowboy act, as well. Eric and Ernie were at the bottom of the bill, below Peter The Equine Marvel, Eddie Ross ('the blackfaced minstrel and his banjo') and a flock of performing pigeons. Ernie was implausibly billed as 'England's Mickey Rooney' and 'the star comedian of the forces' (which was pushing it a bit, on both counts) while Eric had to make do with the more downbeat billing, 'Strike A New Note In Comedy'. Oh well, at least this time they spelt his name right. 'Do not fail to visit the pets corner after the performance,' read the poster, rather plaintively. They'd played the West End, supporting Sid Field. Now they were playing a series of farmers' fields, supporting a llama, a wallaby, a parrot and a troupe of hamsters.

They were able to laugh about it in retrospect, but it didn't seem quite so funny at the time. As well as helping to put up the big top and setting out the seats (all seven hundred of them) they also had to get out and help to sell the show. Eric finally reached breaking point when he was asked to lead Lord Sanger's donkey along the beach at Weymouth with a placard tied to its arse — Saatchi and Saatchi, eat your heart out. It wouldn't have been so bad if they'd been pulling in the punters, but even these advertising gimmicks didn't draw much of a crowd. 'On more than one occasion nobody turned up at all,' recollected Ernie, 'leaving the pair of us marooned in some godforsaken field wearing evening dress and Wellington boots.'[4] The bright lights of the West End felt like a long way away.

Life on the open road made those blitzed-out boarding houses of the war years seem like Claridge's. As their convoy drove along a country lane, their trailer became uncoupled with Eric still inside it. The trailer rolled downhill and finished up upended in a ditch. Luckily, Eric was more shocked than hurt. Anton Petrov did most of the catering, but his cooking wasn't much better than Ernie's. 'The cooking was done over camp fires but there was nothing of a picnic atmosphere about it,'[5] said Eric. Their toilet facilities were equally al

The Nottingham Goose Fair.

fresco — and even less romantic. Their lavatory was a muddy pit behind an old tarpaulin, and on Eric's twenty-first birthday, even this flimsy privacy was denied them, when a mystery joker spiked the sugar with Epsom Salts — a popular (and extremely effective) laxative. As they drove to the next town, vans screeched to a halt as frantic performers ran to relieve themselves in roadside bushes. 'I had to go behind a hedge, in somebody's front garden, in full view of the house,'[6] said Eric. What a way to spend your twenty-first. The culprit remained a mystery, although the boys suspected Anton, who'd been upset by their frank and forthright criticism of his cooking.

Remarkably, in the midst of all this mayhem, Eric and Ernie still found time to develop a few new bits of comic business. One of the sketches they acquired, in which they shared a bed, even anticipated one of their most popular TV routines. Like their TV routine it was completely innocent, and the humour was almost inconsequential — they simply took turns trying (and failing) to blow out their bedtime candle. However they were already learning that, like good sitcoms, the best double acts are about relationships, not jokes. Amid the chaos of Lord Sanger's Circus, it no longer seemed to matter who played the feed and who played the comic, and though Eric never played the feed again, their partnership remained a lot less constrained than most duos who'd never made the swap. As Ernie used to put it, Eric was a comedian who sang and danced a bit, while Ernie was a song-and-dance man who cracked the odd joke. This versatility was central to their subsequent success. Like Laurel and Hardy, they were becoming a double act with two comics – rather than a double act with two straight men, one of whom told gags. However, the mechanics of Morecambe & Wise wasn't the main thing on their minds. As well as his performing animals, Sanger had also hired a dance troupe called The Four Flashes – Betty, Olga, Rose and Ernie's future wife, a pretty fifteen-year-old from Peterborough called Doreen Blythe.

For a girl of fifteen, Doreen already had quite a lot of showbiz savvy. She'd been to ballet school, and danced in local musicals and pantomimes. She'd even travelled down to Devon, to appear in panto in Torquay. The first time Ernie met her, they were eating lunch outside at trestle tables, surrounded by circus caravans. It should have been a romantic setting, but Eric and Ernie didn't know much about romance. Soup was on the menu, and Ernie was cracking jokes about the noises people make when they eat it. Doreen let out a delicate little slurp and Eric and Ernie burst out laughing – inconsequential for a grown-up, but a devastating humiliation for a girl of fifteen. It put Doreen right off soup for years. It also put her right off Ernie. She went bright red and glared at him. 'I fancied her from that second,' said Ernie. 'She was wearing a light-coloured suit which set off her lovely tan.'[7]

Doreen and her friend Rose did their best to avoid Eric and Ernie from then on, but eventually Eric and Ernie cornered them and asked them out to the movies. Gradually, the girls softened. By the end of the tour, Doreen was even washing Ernie's underwear. Rose took to washing Eric's smalls as well (greater love hath no woman) but there wasn't much time left for courting. In October 1947, after a marathon run at Nottingham's annual Goose Fair, Lord John Sanger closed the show, and Eric and Ernie (and Rose and Doreen) went their separate ways. Ernie kept in touch with Doreen, but he didn't keep in touch with Eric. After the shambles of Lord Sanger's Circus, it seemed he might do a lot better on his own.

CHAPTER 10

DOREEN BLYTHE

DOREEN WISE LIVES ALONE in a beautiful house beside the Thames. Her home is down a quiet country lane, surrounded by lush meadows. There are swans and herons on the river, and deer in the woods nearby. It's only fifteen miles from Heathrow. It feels a hundred miles away.

Doreen is sharp and sprightly, with a dancer's poise and posture, but though her smile is warm and welcoming, there's a sadness in her eyes. Ernie died in 1999 and you can tell she still feels his absence keenly. After Eric died, in 1984, Ernie said there was a cold draught down one side of him where Eric used to be. Talking to Doreen, you can sense the same cold draught down one side of her. Ernie was twenty when he met her. Doreen was fifteen. 'It was a fantastic summer,' she says. She was an only child. Ernie was her soulmate. They never had any children. They were together for over fifty years.

We're upstairs, in Ernie's study, looking at his scrapbooks. 'He was such a good-looking fella,' she says, fondly, leafing through these ancient albums, stuffed with old photos and press cuttings. 'He didn't ever take a bad photograph, which we used to hate!' She's right. Eric was a handsome man, but his private snapshots are often diffident and pensive. Ernie, on the other hand, beams out of every frame — happy and untroubled, a man completely comfortable in his own skin. 'We always used to say he should have been a priest,' says Doreen. 'He was placid. He was known as the thin line of sanity.' It was Ernie's sanity which gave shape and form to Eric's daft sense of fun. She shows me photos of Ernie's parents. 'His father could really embarrass you!' What about his mum? 'She was lovely, actually, but she was not an affectionate mother. I only ever saw her put her arms around him once, and that was when Eric died. She just said, "Thank goodness it wasn't you."'

There are photos of Ernie with Jack Hylton and George Black's children, when he was staying with Hylton's family in Angmering-on-Sea. 'That was one of the houses he lived in, right on the beach.' There's even a letter from Hylton to Ernie's parents, written a few days after war was declared, asking if Ernie could stay on in Angmering, rather than returning to Leeds. 'Ernie is staying with me at my house at the seaside,' writes Hylton, on 6 September 1939. 'He is very welcome to stay down there with me and I shall be glad if you will let me know if this is OK, or if you would prefer that he is back home with you. We have six other children there and his being with us does not inconvenience us at all. It is entirely up to you.' There's a letter from Bryan Michie, written to Ernie after he was called up, and had to leave *Strike A New Note* for the merchant navy. 'My dear Ernie, it was so nice to get your letter. Please forgive me for being so long in answering. We missed you very much when you left the show, and I can only hope that you will let me know the moment you are demobbed, and if there is anything going, you shall certainly be in it. Hope you're having not too bad a time and that the family are well. Do let me know when you are next in London.'

Doreen grew up in Peterborough. Her father was an engineer who used to tinkle on the piano. Her mum was a nurse who did some am-dram with the local church. Doreen went to ballet school from the age of four. She played

Doreen joins the boys for some fun in the back garden.

Ernie relaxes by the pool at St Leonards, 1950.

the piano and the violin, which came in handy when she ended up helping Eric and Ernie with the music in their Variety act – all played by a live orchestra in those days, not recorded like it so often is today.

She became good friends with the daughter of the stage manager at the local Variety theatre, the Embassy. He gave them free tickets. They went every Monday night. 'We were in love with Derek Roy, because he wore the blue gabardine suits and he had these big blue eyes!' The Embassy was stunning too. When Doreen started going there, it was still brand-new. A robust slab of art deco, it was the only theatre ever built by the renowned cinema architect, David Evelyn Nye. 'Unprecedented scenes accompanied the opening of Peterborough's magnificent new theatre,' reported the *Peterborough Advertiser* on 5 November 1937. 'The coloured neon lighting, emphasizing the bold lines of its noble outline, projected a glow which could be seen for miles.'

For Ernie, a grown man of twenty, with a couple of West End shows to his name, Lord John Sanger's Circus was a bit of a comedown, but for Doreen, still only fifteen, it was a great adventure. 'I was seeing parts of the country I'd never seen.' Her first impressions of her future husband weren't quite so favourable. 'I didn't like him,' she says. 'I thought he was pushy.' However Ernie was very keen ('I watched those legs going up the stairs and I thought, "I've got to get to know her,"' he recalled, after they were married) and she soon warmed to him. She shows me a photo of the two of them, celebrating her sixteenth birthday. Mind you, there wasn't much time for courting, what with putting out the seats, and selling programmes before the performance.

Once the show ended, it was even harder for Ernie and Doreen to meet up, since they were often in different theatres, in different corners of the country. 'We didn't do weekends together in those days!' The best they could hope for was a hurried rendezvous on a Sunday, between trains at Preston or

Crewe. 'You would always meet other pros, crossing from one platform to another.' It sounds like a lot of fun for singletons, but it's hard to imagine a worse set of circumstances for a long-term romance. But Ernie was a stead-fast boyfriend, and he and Eric both showed the same commitment with their act. 'They were determined that they were going to be successful, and they considered that anybody else didn't know what they were talking about.' They never stopped believing in Morecambe & Wise, and nor did she.

She shows me a Valentine's card from Ernie. He's signed it 'Short Fellow'. 'Looking through these books is most depressing because nearly everybody's gone,' she says. But the odd thing is, looking through these old photos, you realize that Ernie looks just the same at the age of seventy as he did when he was seven. Eric keeps on changing but Ernie hardly changed a bit. 'As I say, you never see a bad picture of him,' she says, proudly. 'When he first died, I wouldn't go out – only at night-time to take the dog out – because every time I met anybody they'd say, "Oh, what a shame about that lovely man!"'

Ernie and Doreen with their beloved pet poodle.

CHAPTER 11

WILSON, KEPPEL AND BETTY

ALTHOUGH ERIC AND ERNIE went their separate ways they both finished up in London. However, they were hardly next-door neighbours. Ernie wound up in south London, lodging with a Japanese acrobat called Kura Izuka in Brixton. Eric ended up in west London, in a guest house in Chiswick with his mum. If it hadn't been for a bizarre twist of fate they might have never worked together again. However just a few days after they arrived in Chiswick, Eric and Sadie were walking down Regent Street when they met Ernie coming the other way. Sadie could see how happy the boys were to see each other again, so she asked Ernie if he'd like to move in with them. 'You two might as well be out of work together as separately,'[1] she told them. Ernie agreed. After all, it was only thirty shillings a week.

Sadie didn't just encourage Eric and Ernie to move back in together. She also encouraged them to revive their apprentice double act. By now they had ten minutes, just about enough for a standard slot on a Variety bill, but they didn't have much luck finding work. It was chicken and egg. To get regular Variety gigs you needed an agent, and an agent wouldn't take you on unless he saw you working. It was no good doing an audition in his office. He'd want to see you in a theatre, in front of a live crowd. Eric and Ernie did their best to break this vicious circle. They tramped up and down Oxford Street, knocking on agents' doors, but all to no avail. Usually, they couldn't even get past

Right **An early portrait of Eric's mother, Sadie.**

Opposite **Seeing Wilson, Keppel & Betty perform their hugely popular act certainly rubbed off on the young double act. Eric and Ernie did their own tribute to them in their BBC show with actress-turned-politician Glenda Jackson playing the part of Betty.**

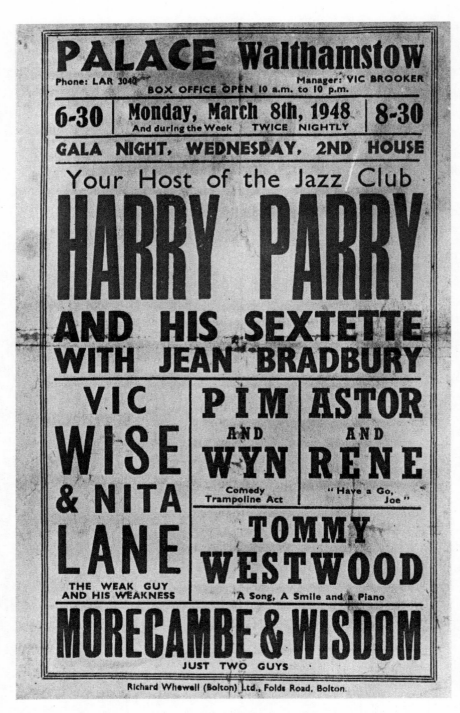

To avoid confusion, promoters changed Ernie's name to Wisdom lest the audience think that Vic had replaced him.

the secretary. Understandably, such rejection left them with a jaundiced view of agents – well, most of them, at least. 'Most Variety agents of that period had started in show business as bad acts,' said Eric. 'They had realized they could not survive as pros so they would survive on pros.'[2] But that realization was no comfort. If anything, it made things even worse.

Defeated and downhearted, they often finished up at the Express Dairy café on Charing Cross Road, where 'resting' entertainers would congregate between jobs, to swap news and gossip. A lot of these acts would be going on about some brilliant booking they had lined up, but they'd still spin out a cup of coffee from ten o'clock in the morning to four o'clock in the afternoon. 'Everything seemed to depend on the agent, who must be wooed and placated,' said Eric. 'To my way of thinking it should be the other way around.'[3] But no one else seemed to think so. By now they were in their early twenties. They weren't child stars any more.

Yet Eric and Ernie were made of sterner stuff than most of the dreamers in the Express Dairy. They decided to forget about the agents for a while, and go straight to the booking managers who ran the theatres. It was an uphill struggle, but they picked up a few bits and pieces. They got £25 for a week in Cardiff, £14 for a week in Bournemouth, and finally, in 1948, they landed a week at the Palace Theatre in Walthamstow, from the eighth to the sixteenth of March. Harry Parry's Jazz Sextette was the headline act, supported by Tommy Westwood ('a song, a smile and a piano') and a trampoline duo called Pim and Wyn. However there was also a comedian on the bill with the same surname as Ernie (Vic Wise, a comic in his late forties who'd started out in South Africa before the First World War, billed as 'The World's Youngest Magician') so, to avoid any confusion, Eric and Ernie were billed as Morecambe and Wisdom. As it turned out, they were glad of the disguise. Their East End audience were singularly unimpressed, and the booker who'd given them this big break never booked them again. Stardom was still a long way off.

Throughout the fourteen months they lived in Chiswick, Eric and Ernie spent less than six weeks in work. Unemployment has always been an occupational hazard of showbusiness, and even the biggest stars knew that whenever you most needed a break, you could be sure you were least likely to get one. As the great Max Miller told them, in 1948, 'In this business, when

An early panto performance reminiscent of speciality act, Wilson, Keppel and Betty.

Eric and Ernie pay their own tribute to Wilson, Keppel and Betty, rehearsing here with Glenda Jackson for a sketch on their 1971 television show.

one door shuts, they all bloody shut!'[4] They were lucky that their landlady wasn't the dragon of popular mythology, but an unusually understanding woman called Eleanor Duer. 'Pay me when you're back in funds,'[5] she used to tell them, even though the gaps between their engagements often stretched to several months. Her husband was a similarly kindly soul. Mr Duer treated Eric and Ernie like members of his own family – a bit like Jack Hylton, but on a more modest scale. He'd take them out for day trips on his motorbike, along the Thames to Runnymede. Eric rode pillion. Ernie sat in the sidecar. The only concession they had to make to the Duers' more solvent guests was to vacate their favourite armchairs, and let them sit beside the fire.

One reason why Nell Duer was so sympathetic to their plight was that many of her other guests were Variety artistes, since she lived just around the corner from the Chiswick Empire. Built in 1912 by the legendary Frank Matcham, this splendid theatre was sadly demolished in 1959 and replaced by a boring office block, but back then it was one of London's finest Variety theatres, and although Eric and Ernie didn't stand a hope in hell of getting on the same bill as the acts who played there, at least they could share a chinwag with them at Mrs Duer's after the show. The Variety acts they met there included Paul Kafka, an American trapeze artiste who walked a high wire pulled taut between the teeth of two concrete-jawed assistants. His badly fitting toupee inspired Eric's famous running gag, 'You can't see the join,' leading millions of people to assume (quite incorrectly) that Ernie wore a wig.

Another act they met at Mrs Duer's was one of the Variety circuit's most eccentric – and successful – speciality acts, Wilson, Keppel and Betty. Their act was ridiculously simple, and wonderfully funny – an Egyptian sand dance, performed in fezzes and white nightshirts, with Betty as Cleopatra. It wasn't remotely authentic, and it was all the funnier for it. Joe Wilson came from Cork, Jack Keppel was a Scouser and Betty Knox was an American who'd been in a double act with Jack Benny. Their act was completely silent and consequently completely international. They toured throughout Europe, and were even a big hit in Nazi Germany, although Dr Josef Goebbels said their bare legs were 'bad for the morals of the Nazi Youth'.[6] After their show at Berlin's Wintergarten, he suggested they wear long trousers. Thankfully, they never listened to his advice. By the time Jack and Joe met Eric and Ernie, they'd been doing the act for nearly forty years – they started way back in 1910 – and were already on their third Betty (the first Betty made way for her daughter, Betty Junior, in 1932, who made way for her own daughter, Patsy, in 1941). Jack and Joe soldiered on until 1963. 'They had always made good money and never seemed to spend much,' said Ernie. 'They must have left a fortune.'[7] Eric and Ernie's own sand dance, performed on TV, with Glenda Jackson as Cleopatra, was a fitting tribute to this classic act.

CHAPTER 12

THE WINDMILL
STEEPLECHASE

ERIC AND ERNIE FINALLY FOUND some gainful employment at London's Windmill Theatre. It was a far cry from playing the Chiswick Empire alongside Wilson, Keppel and Betty, but it was £25 for a week's work, with an option of five more weeks to follow. The Windmill was in the heart of the West End, but it was hardly the London Palladium. Loads of comics played here on the way up, including Barry Cryer, Dick Emery, Harry Secombe and Peter Sellers, but they were merely window-dressing. The main attraction was the nudes.

The Windmill was the creation of an elderly and wealthy widow called Laura Henderson, (who would later find fame of her own when portrayed by Judi Dench in the movie *Mrs Henderson Presents*). In 1931 Mrs Henderson bought the old Palais de Luxe cinema in Great Windmill Street in Soho, and converted it into a tiny theatre. At first she put on straight plays but they lost money, and in 1932 her new theatre manager Vivian Van Damm (played by Bob Hoskins in the movie) came up with the bright idea of staging a daily Variety show called Revuedeville – not twice nightly, like most Variety shows, but non-stop from 2.30 p.m. to 11 p.m.

For the first few years, Revuedeville employed the usual Light Ent mix of singers, dancers and entertainers, but the Windmill was still losing money, so in 1937 Van Damm introduced his first nudes. This was rather daring, since in those days the theatres were still overseen by the Lord Chamberlain, an archaic royal flunkey with the power to censor any theatrical performance – a power he retained right up until the Theatres Act of 1968.

The Lord Chamberlain didn't wield his authority lightly. *Goon Show* legend Michael Bentine, who played the Windmill a few years before Eric and Ernie, summed up his vicelike grip on all of the performing arts: 'The multiple prohibitions, restrictions and penalizations, including heavy fines and even

imprisonment, were intended to suppress or eliminate blasphemy, obscenity (both in language and actions), lewdness, unlicensed performances under the influence of alcohol, exploitation of child performers, cruelty to performing animals, immorality (both on and off the stage, but within the confines of the theatre), and any other "criminal" acts, both real or imaginary.'[1] It was a wonder anyone managed to put on any shows at all.

However, Van Damm discovered an ingenious loophole in this tangle of red tape. The Lord Chamberlain's restrictions only applied to performance, and so naked actors (or actresses) were exempt so long as they didn't move. As the old song went, 'it's all right to be nude, but if it moves it's rude'.[2] Van Damm was careful not to stray beyond the limits of this surreal ruling. When one of his nude girls had a coughing fit (to tumultuous applause) he quickly brought the curtain down. And to make sure the Lord Chamberlain would raise no objections, VD (as he became known, affectionately or otherwise) invited his Lordship along to the opening night of each new show. As Nicholas Parsons, another Windmill veteran, noted wryly, 'the fact that the Lord Chamberlain never delegated his responsibility to an underling on these occasions suggested that he did not find the visits irksome.'[3] However, his Lordship didn't see quite the same show as subsequent paying punters. 'Girls who would normally be rather economically clad would be covered in yards of tulle and flimsy lace,' remembered Parsons. 'It would be six weeks before he would be seen again at the Windmill. It would also be six weeks before the tulle and flimsy lace were seen again.'[4]

Even without any tulle or lace these shows were terribly twee by modern standards, but for Eric and Ernie's generation it seemed like pretty racy stuff. Somehow, Van Damm managed to make the Windmill seem both respectable and risqué – tame enough to reassure the Lord Chamberlain and his cronies, sufficiently saucy to attract a paying crowd. In actual fact, there was hardly any total nudity. It was mostly just tit and bum.

Mrs Laura Henderson added a high-society gloss to this veneer of bourgeois respectability. She invited celebrities to see the show, even members of the Royal Family. Queen Victoria's daughter and granddaughter (Helena Victoria and Marie Louise) both came along. However, the Windmill's own house rules provide a better indication of the clientele these shows attracted. Cameras and binoculars were forbidden, though one ingenious punter got inside with a set of homemade binoculars that looked just like jam jar specs. (Although they gave him a great view of the stage, he could hardly see in front of him. He fell down the stairs and broke his leg. The staff confiscated his telescopic spectacles until the ambulance arrived.)

Climbing across the seats was also strictly prohibited, but this rule was a lot harder to enforce. Naturally, the Windmill's mackintosh-clad regulars liked to sit as close to the stage as possible, and since the show ran six times a day, without a break, from 10 a.m. until 10 p.m., as soon as one punter got up to go, the punter behind him would clamber over the seat in front to take his place. Although it was against the rules this practice became so commonplace that it acquired its own nickname, the Windmill Steeplechase. 'The small, packed audience were mostly regular and dedicated voyeurs,' remembered Bentine. 'Many of them had noticeable erections, which they handled during the nude tableaux. They were usually spotted by the nudes. As soon as the girls were offstage, they would inform the stage manager, "Row three, seat six, elderly grey-haired gent. He's at it. Dirty old man."'[5]

Needless to say, these one-handed enthusiasts weren't particularly interested in stand-up comedy, and although any pocket billiard players were rapidly ejected by the management, even those spectators who kept their hands out of their trousers were pretty indifferent to the comics. Plenty of punters simply opened their newspapers when the comedian came on.

Marketing, not stage management, was where Van Damm's talent lay. 'We never closed' read the sign outside the Windmill after the war, as if putting on a nude revue had been a vital contribution to the war effort. 'We never clothed' quipped the comics, but neither slogan was entirely true. The Windmill was forced to close for twelve days at the start of the war, just like all the other theatres, and as Nicholas Parsons pointed out, anyone who came here expecting a feast of full frontal nudity might well have had a case for the Office of Fair Trading.

Van Damm had a flair for publicity but he didn't really have an eye for comedy. He booked a lot of future stars, but like a million monkeys typing Shakespeare, that was really just the law of averages. He employed so many comics (there was a pretty rapid turnover) that some of them were bound to hit the big time in the end. He gave Jimmy Edwards his first break, but he turned down Benny Hill, Spike Milligan and Norman Wisdom. He hired Bruce Forsyth but he told Nicholas Parsons that he thought Forsyth would never make it.

Even Van Damm's auditions left quite a bit to be desired. To get a booking at the Windmill, you had to perform infront of him – not onstage but in his office. No reaction, no applause – just a yes or a no and that was that.

Against all odds, some entertainers prospered. Upper-class comic Gillie Potter went down well, in his blazer and straw boater. So did bumbling Yorkshireman Harry Worth, and future sitcom star Arthur English – aka Mr Harman, the caretaker in *Are You Being Served?* Percy Edwards got a few laughs with his wonderful animal impressions. A Fellow of the Royal Zoological Society, he could imitate over a hundred different birdsongs, but his ornithological talents were wasted on this onanistic audience, who were merely waiting for their next pound of female flesh. Jimmy Edwards did best of all, with his confrontational sense of fun, but Eric and Ernie's boyish humour was

totally unsuited to this lewd revue. As they waited in the wings on Monday, one of the dancers asked Eric for a light. She was stark naked. Eric's hand shook as he lit her fag. 'You silly billy,' she said. 'After you've been here six weeks you won't turn a hair.' 'It will have all fallen out,' said Eric.[6] They walked on to the sound of their own footsteps, and off to the same sound ten minutes later. Nothing they said could raise a smile from these men with rain-coats across their knees, and they were booked to do six shows a day.

Things were just as bad on Tuesday, and when they turned up for work on Wednesday they were called into Van Damm's office. VD had decided to replace them with another double act, Derek Scott and Tony Hancock – soon to become a household name in *Hancock's Half Hour*, but just another jobbing comic back then. They could play on until Saturday, but that was their lot. It was a bitter blow. They didn't like performing here, but they could have done with a few more weeks at £25 a week, and they'd already told several agents they'd be here for the next six weeks, in the hope that some of them might come and see them and agree to take them on.

This setback could have broken them. Instead it was their making. Despite their disappointment, Ernie had the presence of mind to ask Van Damm if they could put an advert in *The Stage*, saying they were leaving due to prior com-mitments, by mutual consent. Of course there was nothing mutual about it, and they had no other commitments whatsoever, but Ernie didn't want the Variety world to know that they'd been fired. In fact, the Variety world didn't give a damn either way, but this advertisement gave them the Dutch courage to sit down and write to twenty agents and invite them to the show. Nobody turned up on Thursday and nobody turned up Friday, but on Saturday, their last day, an agent called Gordon Norval came along. Van Damm wouldn't give him a ticket so Eric and Ernie had to fork out thirteen shillings for a box. It was money they could ill afford to spend, but their investment paid off. The next day, out of work again, they went along to Norval's office on Charing Cross Road. This time they weren't fobbed off by a secretary. 'Can you do the Clapham Grand on Monday?' asked Norval. Ernie leafed through his empty diary. 'I think we might just be free that night,' he replied.[7]

Opposite and overleaf **The Winter Gardens, Morecambe played host to some of the greatest comedy double acts of the twentieth century: not only Morecambe & Wise but also their heroes Laurel and Hardy and Abbott and Costello.**

99

WINTER GARDENS

MORECAMBE.

| Director ... ... C. A. INGRAM | General Manager - LOUIS BENJAMIN |

Manager ... ... JAMES PITMAN

TELEPHONE NUMBERS:

Booking Office - Morecambe 8   General Office - Morecambe 1114
Stage Door - - Morecambe 1842   Restaurant - - Morecambe 677

NEXT WEEK   6-15 — Twice Nightly — 8-30

"Britain's New Singing Star"   "The Glamourous Television Star"
DAVID WHITFIELD   KAREN GREER

"Jest Artistes"
FREDDIE BAMBERGER & PAM

and, an All Star Supporting Company

NEXT SUNDAY, at 7-30

JACK PARNELL AND HIS MUSIC MAKERS

FOR THREE DAYS ONLY—
MONDAY, TUESDAY & WEDNESDAY, AUG 24th, 25th & 26th.

PERSONAL APPEARANCE
OF
BUD ABBOTT & LOU COSTELLO

BOOK NOW TO AVOID DISAPPOINTMENT

WINTER GARDENS
MORECAMBE.
Proprietors: THE WINTER GARDENS (MORECAMBE & HEYSHAM) LTD

Joint Managing Directors:	Manager ... EDWARD COPUS
J. W. CARLETON & H. SMIRK·	Secretary ... ... C. A. INGRAM

TELEPHONE NUMBERS:
Morecambe 8 — Booking Office.   Morecambe 1114 — General Office.
Morecambe 1842 — Stage Door.   Morecambe 677 — Restaurant.

WEEK COMMENCING MONDAY, MAY 26th, 1947.
TWICE NIGHTLY AT 6-0 AND 8-10.

BERNARD DELFONT Presents

LAUREL & HARDY
In Variety

1.	REG FISHER AND HIS MUSIC	
2.	THE THREE REDHEADS	Dancing To Delight
3.	JOHNSON CLARKE	Sportsman Ventriloquist
4.	SLIM RHYDER	Komedy Kapers
5.	CONNIE GRAHAM & HAL SCOTT	The STAR Comedienne
6.	NEWMAN TWINS	Sensational Acrobatic Stars
7.	INTERVAL	
	REG FISHER AND HIS MUSIC	
8.	THE THREE REDHEADS	More Steps In Rhythm
9.	CONNIE GRAHAM & HAL SCOTT	Here's Fun Again
10.	MACKENZIE REID & DOROTHY	Moments Of Melody
11.	STAN LAUREL & OLIVER HARDY	
	Hollywood's Greatest Comedy Couple	
12.	OLGA VARONA	Australia's Queen of the Air

WINTER GARDENS

MORECAMBE

General Manager: Louis Benjamin

Asst. General Manager: James Pitman   Manager: Roy Armitage

Musical Director: Reg Fisher

TELEPHONE NUMBERS

Booking Office ... ... Morecambe 8   General Office ... ... Morecambe 1114
Stage Door ... ... Morecambe 1842   Restaurant ... ... Morecambe 677

BOX OFFICE OPEN 9.30 a.m. to 9 p.m.

─────── 6.15   Twice Nightly   8.30 ───────

BERNARD DELFONT presents the Star-studded Resident Summer Revue

"LIGHT UP THE TOWN"

Staged by MAURICE FOURNIER   Dance Ensembles by REG DREW

1. **OVERTURE**

2. **THE SAME OLD BLACK MAGIC** (Phil Park) The George Mitchell Singers
   (a) **Minstrel Days** (1900) .... The Dancing Girls
   (b) **Red Plush, Gaslight & Tights** (1910) .... Nancy Munks
   (c) **Musical Comedy** (1916) .... KEN PLATT & AUDREY MANN
   (d) **Revue** (1958) .... The Company

3. **FOOLS RUSH IN** .... **MORECAMBE AND WISE**

4. **WHITE SOMBRERO** .... AUDREY MANN, George Mitchell Singers
   and The Girls

   Introducing " Music & Movement " ...... THE KENDOR BROTHERS

5. **MIXED DOUBLES** (Green & Hills) .... **KEN PLATT**
   The Customers .... Molly & Nancy Monks

6. **YOU'RE ONLY YOUNG ONCE!** .... **MORECAMBE AND WISE**

7. **OLD ONES, NEW ONES, LOVED ONES, NEGLECTED ONES**
   SEMPRINI

I N T E R M I S S I O N

The Winter Gardens Orchestra under the direction of REG FISHER

8. **GYMNASIUM ROMP** .... The Dancing Lovelies

9. **LEASE-LEND** .... **MORECAMBE AND WISE, AUDREY MANN**,
   Molly Munks

FULLY LICENSED BARS IN ALL PARTS OF THEATRE
Port and Sherry 2/.   Beers and Minerals at popular prices.   Whisky 2/1.   Gin 2/1

CHAPTER 13

FIG LEAVES AND APPLE SAUCE

ERIC AND ERNIE WERE BOOKED to do two ten-minute slots at the Clapham Grand. However they only had ten minutes of material, and that had taken them nearly ten years to put together. Now they had to write another ten minutes in one week. They wrote down every gag they could recall, from old Abbott and Costello movies right back to the comics they'd worked with in *Youth Takes A Bow*. However that still left them several minutes short, so they worked out a bit of nonsense around a popular Danny Kaye number called 'The Woody Woodpecker Song' ('he pecks a few holes in a tree, to see if a redwood's really red, and it's nothing to him, on the tiniest whim, to peck a few holes in your head'). The flimsy premise of this sketch was that Ernie promised Eric the leading role, then left him with just a few notes to sing. It was a lot of build-up for not much pay-off and they didn't have very high hopes for it, but they couldn't afford to leave it out. They had nothing else.

The show was called *Fig Leaves and Apple Sauce*. As its title implied, it was another nude revue, but at least it was in a proper Variety theatre, in front of a proper Variety crowd. Eric and Ernie were due to go on second in each half — traditionally the two toughest spots. They decided to do their tried-and-tested act in the first half, in the hope of building up a bit of goodwill for the hastily assembled second routine they'd worked up the week before. It didn't quite work out like that. 'We stood there motionless with glazed looks trying to gabble out our words while our mouths got drier and drier,' recalled Ernie.[1] They walked off to the notorious 'Clapham Silence'. It was a nervous wait backstage, killing time until their second spot. They'd already died with

This colourful drawing by Bill Wright introduces a fresh new act on the scene. Note the reference to the 'Woody Woodpecker song', which played such a big part in getting Morecambe & Wise on to the Variety circuit.

the best material. Now they had to go back on in front of the same blank faces, and do ten minutes of brand-new stuff. To their amazement, this fresh stuff ripped the roof off. They'd discovered that a good double act is more like sit-com than stand-up comedy. It's about the immediacy and the intimacy of the relationship. It isn't really about the jokes at all.

On the strength of this barnstormer, they got a week's work at the Kilburn Empire. By the time they returned to Clapham the week after that, they'd switched their two ten-minute spots around. It was a smart move. After 'The Woody Woodpecker Song', audiences were far more inclined to laugh at their corny one-liners, and Eric and Ernie were able to deliver these old chestnuts with the chutzpah they required. 'Failure generated fear and fear generated paralysis,'[2] reflected Ernie, looking back on the many times they'd died. Now that process was reversed. Comedy is a confidence trick. It's all about self-belief. Audiences can smell terror. They can smell self-assurance too. If a comic acts like he expects to get laughs, he usually tends to get them. When they went back to Kilburn a week later, they were top of the bill.

By now Ernie was going steady with Doreen Blythe, the pretty young dancer he'd met at Lord Sanger's Circus. Doreen was touring with a show run by a xylophone-player called Reggie Dennis, and she persuaded Reggie to come and see the boys at the Clapham Grand. Reggie liked what he saw. He invited them to join his touring revue, *Front Page Personalities*. Eric and Ernie were thrilled. The headline act was the celebrated mindreader Maurice Fogel who also caught bullets in his teeth. There was a trampoline act called the Kovaks, and the obligatory stripper. Reggie played his xylophone and his wife Sylvia sang some songs. The show toured for eleven months on the 'Number Two' circuit – not as big or smart as the 'Number One' venues (the Stoll Theatres, the Butterworths and the Moss Empires) but decent theatres nonetheless. When the show came to London they played the Metropolitan Edgware Road. This was the venue all up-and-coming comics dreamt of playing – and not just because it was one of the few Variety theatres where you could watch the show from the bar. A music hall since 1836, it had been rebuilt by Frank Matcham in 1897, in especially palatial style. Tragically, it was torn down in 1963 to make way for a new motorway, confirming that old adage that town planners did more damage to London than the Luftwaffe.

Touring with Reggie Dennis in *Front Page Personalities* really taught the boys their trade. 'We learnt how to go on and do a few extra minutes off the top, the very thought of which had previously scared us rigid,' said Ernie. 'We learnt how to compère and introduce acts, to go out and get a laugh on just local gags and chat.'[3] Inspired by Syd and Max Harrison, a popular double act during the 1930s and 1940s, Eric and Ernie developed an up-tempo style, rather than the traditional step-pause-gag delivery, with built-in breaks for laughs. This was when they dreamed up that face-slapping routine that became a hallmark of their TV shows. They'd sing some songs, do a few pratfalls and a tap-dance and tell dozens of dreadful gags. These were the same old hand-me-down one-liners, no better than before, but the jokes weren't so important, now that they'd acquired a personality, and a point of view.

Their big break finally came through two acrobats called Jock Cochrane and Reggie Dennis (aka The Two Pirates) whom they'd met at Mrs Duer's. Jock and Reggie kindly recommended them to Frank Pope, an agent who had the ear of the bookers for the Butterworth and Moss Empire theatres. If you could get on to these two circuits, you'd be gigging regularly in some of the best Variety venues in the land. Pope went to Grimsby to see them do a show (he must have been pretty keen) and signed them up at a guaranteed £10 a week. After a decade in the business, they were a proper Variety act at last. The first gig he got for them was supporting Josef Locke, a Londonderry tenor who'd served in the Irish Guards, the Palestine Police and the Royal Ulster Constabulary – hence his nickname, The Singing Bobby. The venue was the Swansea Empire, where the boys first met eleven years before. Those first eleven years had been a long and arduous apprenticeship, but it would be another eleven years before they landed a successful TV series of their own.

Above **Eric discovers what fun he can have now he's acquired his trademark dark horn-rimmed glasses.**

Opposite and right **He's behind you! Eric and Ernie onstage during their pantomime years.**

Eric backstage with friends and colleagues
during Morecambe & Wise's panto years.

CHAPTER 14

VOGELBEIN'S BEARS

ERIC AND ERNIE WERE NOW MEMBERS of a select club, the Moss Empire circuit. If the Variety circuit was like the Football League, the Moss Empire circuit was the Premiership – two dozen first-class theatres, presenting Variety every week, twice nightly and three times on Saturdays. When the boys signed on with Frank Pope, there were hundreds of Variety theatres in Britain, and the Moss Empires were the venues every entertainer yearned to play. Little did they know it, but this was actually Variety's last hurrah. During the 1950s over 400 Variety theatres would close. What made Eric and Ernie (and their TV shows) so special was that they were the last double act to play this circuit in its prime.

Like a large fleet of well-oiled and opulently furnished ocean liners, the Moss Empires gave no indication that Variety's days were numbered. Just like the ocean liners, it seemed these theatres would always be around. They were run with almost military precision by an intimidating little Londoner called Cissie Williams. She'd see all the new acts at the Finsbury Park Empire – the closest Moss Empire to London's West End, since the Holborn Empire was bombed during the Blitz. If she liked what she saw, she'd send them out on tour. As second-spot comics (straight after the opening dance act – a tall order on any bill) Eric and Ernie were paid £35 a week, plus £10 for the Glasgow Empire – ostensibly for the train fare, but mainly as danger money. Yet they'd come a long way since their first trip to the English comics' graveyard in 1941, in only their second performance as a double act, in *Youth Takes A Bow*. This time the headline act was the Jewish singer (and joker) Issy Bonn (born Benny Levin) and singers usually went down pretty well in Glasgow. Bonn was born in London, but his kosher heritage gave his act a more Yiddish than English flavour, and the warm reception he received from this fierce crowd rubbed off on the boys.

Eric and Ernie appeared with all sorts of acts, and learnt what really moved an audience, as they watched from the wings. The juggler Henri Vadden had an especially spectacular (and effective) finale. He'd finish his act by spinning a cartwheel above his head, impaled on the spike of an old Prussian helmet. It must have been a right old nuisance lugging a cartwheel around the country, and over the course of his long career this stunt shortened his neck by several inches. Nevertheless it brought the house down, and while you were onstage, in front of a paying crowd, that was really all that counted. The boys were happy to 'borrow' material from their fellow entertainers, but this was one routine they didn't filch. Ernie was short enough already.

The old playbills for these theatres read like a 'Who's Who' of Variety. They toured with bandleaders like Ray Ellington, and Phyllis Dixey, the Queen of Striptease. They worked with some wonderful singers, too: Eve Boswell, a South African who could sing in eleven different languages; Ruby Murray, who had five simultaneous singles in the hit parade (still a record) and Alma Cogan, 'the girl with the giggle in her voice' who died of cancer, aged just thirty-four. It's strange to scan these playbills, knowing now what lay in store for these artistes. Most of these headline acts are long forgotten, while Eric and Ernie, at the bottom of every bill, ended up as household names.

MORECAMBE & WISE

And then there were the speciality acts: trick cyclists, tightrope walkers, knife throwers and fire eaters. There was a ventriloquist called James Tattersall who worked with life-sized clockwork dummies. They were remarkably realistic. Tattersall made them himself. 'They breathed, they walked about,' said Ernie. 'I wouldn't be surprised if they even had a bit on the side.'[1]

There were also lots of animal acts, like Duncan's Collies, a troupe of border collies who played a football match onstage, dressed in coloured, numbered jerseys. They dribbled the ball with their noses. The goalies were on leads, so they couldn't come too far out of goal. There was the odd off-the-ball incident, and the ball sometimes ended up in the orchestra pit, but most of the dogs were skilful dribblers (their passing left a bit more to be desired) and as far as anyone could tell, they seemed to enjoy it just as much as the audience. And the audience loved it, greeting every goal with a huge cheer.

The most extraordinary animal act of all was Hans Vogelbein's performing bears. Hans taught them to balance on balls and ride around on bicycles, but they were always muzzled. They were dangerous, but Hans knew how to handle them. This huge German loved his bears and they loved him in return. When he went into hospital they wouldn't eat, and when he came out they were in such bad shape that he was told they'd have to be put down. Hans shot them himself, his cheeks wet with tears.

After that ordeal Hans didn't want to work with bears again, so he trained a chimp called Gilbert. Hans would come on with Gilbert, hand in hand, and give him his cues by squeezing his hand. Again and again, Gilbert would interrupt the show to bend down and peer through a gap between the floorboards. It was a great running gag. 'Down there is the chorus girls' dressing-room,'[2] Hans would tell the audience. Who said the Germans had no sense of humour? Backstage Gilbert would unwind by smoking a cigarette in the dressing-room, with his feet up on the table. After Gilbert retired, Hans told his friends he knew it was time to pack it in when Gilbert started giving Hans the cues by squeezing Hans's hand.

Eric and Ernie resumed their old touring routine, a familiar feature of their daily lives ever since their wartime debut in *Youth Takes A Bow*. On Sunday they'd pack up their troubles and travel to the next town on their itinerary. This usually meant a long train journey, invariably with a change at Crewe. On Sunday evening (or Sunday afternoon if they were lucky) they'd find a friendly boarding house and settle in. Monday morning was band call, when the acts would rehearse their music with the orchestra. The acts would place their band books along the edge of the stage, as close to the conductor's podium as possible. As soon as you'd been through your score with the band you were free to go, so the conductor would go through the scores in strict rotation. Only the headline act was allowed to jump the queue.

Variety artistes received cinema tickets, as part of a reciprocal arrangement between the theatres and the cinemas, so in the afternoon they'd see a movie, then return to the theatre at about 6 p.m. and find their dressing-rooms. These were usually pretty basic. Unless you were a headline act they were hardly ever en suite. There'd be a sign that read, 'Ladies – Please Do Not Wash Off Your Wet White In The Sink.'[3] Wet White was a kind of make-up, but the sign also had another meaning. It also meant, 'Gentlemen – Please Refrain From Pissing In The Sink,' yet since the nearest khazi was often a few floors down, most gentlemen carried on regardless.

'It could be quite a lonely life,' recalled Ernie. 'Arriving half an hour before curtain up, dressing, doing the make-up and hearing the plaintive sound of the band tuning up. That could be a pretty sad sound when we were stuck in some provincial second-rate joint doing medium to bad business on a cold and wet Monday evening.'[4] Monday was the toughest night – local land-ladies on free tickets. When punters get something for nothing, they always suspect it can't be much good. If you could make these battleaxes laugh, you knew you must be doing something right. Their word of mouth could make or break a show, so it was important to try and entertain them. As Eric said, if they didn't like it you didn't do good business.

Tuesday morning was always tense. The cast would meet in the local Kardomah coffee house, to read the overnight reviews. If the notices were bad it would be hard to lift the show that night. The Wednesday matinée was a tough show too. It was half-day closing and the theatre would be full of local shopkeepers on free tickets – a quid pro quo for putting a poster in their shop windows. 'Half-day closing is murder,' Eric used to say. 'The shopkeepers think they are sophisticated.'[5] Audiences are always loath to laugh if they haven't paid for the privilege. And anyway, this hardbitten bunch had seen it all before.

Thursday was easier – the end of the week was in sight, for the performers and the punters. Friday night was even better, Saturday afternoon was better still, and Saturday night – well, if you couldn't make them laugh on a Saturday night you were probably in the wrong business. The other acts would go out after the last show and drink away their wages, but it was never Eric and Ernie's style to piss their hard-earned money up the wall. Instead, they'd go back to their boarding house and sit up talking until the small hours, dreaming and planning, dreaming and planning, too wired to go to sleep. They weren't drinkers, and they weren't womanizers either. Ernie was going steady with Doreen, though since she was a Variety artiste herself, he didn't get much chance to see her. 'The Variety days were great because it was like a sort of club,' says Doreen. 'You'd meet people one week and then you'd say, "Where are you working next week? Oh, we'll see you at the end of the month, then."' That was fine for friends, but not much use for courting. 'When we had time to chase girls we didn't have the money, and when we had the money we were working so hard we never had the time,'[6] said Eric, but in 1952, at the Edinburgh Empire, he met the woman who would change his life.

CHAPTER 15

JOAN BARTLETT

JOAN MORECAMBE IS SITTING on the patio of her handsome family home in Harpenden, which she bought with Eric in 1967, just before his first heart attack. 'Eric could always imagine growing old with me,' she says. 'He was going to be this fella with a straw hat on and pince-nez, and I was going to be this tall, upright elegant lady who went about with a rose basket on her arm.' Sadly, there's no knowing what Eric would have been like as an old man, but apart from the rose basket, his vision of his wife was spot-on.

Joan lives alone here now, as she has done since Eric died, although her son and daughter, Gary and Gail, and her adopted son, Steven, often come to stay. Gail was fourteen when they moved here. Gary was eleven. They're both in their fifties now, with families of their own. We're sitting in the back garden, beside the fish pond. Beyond the garden is a golf course, and beyond that, open fields. 'Golf is a wonderful sport,' Eric used to say, 'especially if your wife won't let you drink at home.' He was only joking. He played a few rounds now and then, but he far preferred fishing and bird-watching. Joan must be nearly eighty now, but she's still slim and striking. It's no surprise she was a beauty queen (Miss Kent and Miss Margate, to be precise) though that was before she met Eric, over half a century ago.

'People loved Eric and Ernie,' she says. 'They didn't just like them. They didn't just laugh at them, as they do at a lot of comics now. They'll laugh at them and think they're terribly funny – they don't actually love them. But with Eric and Ernie, it was almost like you went into their home. You were

Joan shows off some of the many qualities which earned her the title of Miss Kent and Miss Margate, and which captured the heart of her future husband.

117

Joan is crowned Miss Kent and Miss Margate 1951.

part of their family. This is why when Eric died people were actually in mourning. It was like losing one of their family. You don't get that very often.' This plush but unpretentious house was Eric's refuge, and the family home that Joan made here was his sanctuary. 'We all kept his feet on the ground.'

Eric met the love of his life in the summer of 1952 at the Edinburgh Empire. It's called the Festival Theatre today, but behind the modern glass façade, the old auditorium is still there. It was here that they first set eyes on one another, at the Monday morning band call. For him, it was love at first sight, but not for her. For one thing, she already had a boyfriend. And for another thing, she was feeling far too glum to fall in love. She'd done some dancing and a few bit parts, but she really wanted to be a singer, not a chorus girl or a comic's feed, and she thought she was on her way when Lew and Leslie Grade took her on. She'd spent six months working up an act, and she'd spent £180 on costumes (more like £1800 today) but despite two of Britain's best showbiz promoters behind her, her solo career hadn't taken off. She was living in digs in London, still waiting for her big break, when Lew sent her all the way to Edinburgh, a place she'd never been before, to replace a girl who'd gone down with appendicitis. 'He wanted someone in a hurry,' she says. 'It was just a walk-on part. I had to look very glamorous and that was about it. I only had one line to learn.' It was better than nothing, but she could sense her chance of stardom had already come and gone.

Like a lot of young female entertainers who weren't in quite the right place at quite the right time, Joan looked bound for a workaday career as a soubrette – a Variety all-rounder, able to sing a bit and dance a bit and deliver the odd line. 'You had to be able to do bits and pieces. You had to be willing to slot into the show to do all the odd bits that were needed. You might do a song yourself, which was always a bit of a thrill, that you actually had a number for yourself, and you toured week after week.'

And so when she got to Edinburgh, she fell into the familiar weekly routine. 'You'd get up late, you'd go to the theatre in the morning to see if there was any mail, or any messages for you. You'd see the stage doorkeeper, and he'd hand you your mail. And then, if there were other people about, doing the same thing, invariably you'd say, "Would you like to go and have a coffee?"' Eric was at the theatre, checking his mail, and he asked Joan out for a coffee straight away. 'People think I'm making it up, but he actually did say to the girl who introduced us, "That's the girl I'm going to marry." Everyone used to laugh and say, "They should put a plaque there, saying "Eric Morecambe fell here."' He proposed to her that week. 'He told me he was going to marry me. I said, "Oh no you're not. I don't know you." I was flattered but I was very taken aback. But I liked him.'

She liked the act as well. 'I watched it from the wings and it was the first time I'd ever seen them. I instantly thought, "They can't fail. They've got to be a big success." I never even doubted it. They were very, very funny, and I never ever saw them fail with an audience.' And back then they were playing the dreaded second spot, warming up the audience after the opening dance act. Once they were offstage, she started to notice the differences between them. Eric was very highly strung, Ernie was much more placid, but they were friends as well as colleagues, with the same sense of humour. And like all the

Four of a kind: Eric and Ernie with Joan Morecambe (left) and Doreen Wise (right).

best double acts, their main aim was always to make each other laugh. 'Eric and Ernie were great fun,' she says. 'You'd pass their dressing-room door and there were always hoots of laughter. They were very carefree, a happy-go-lucky couple of fellas.' Yet even in those early days, there was resolve behind the laughter. 'They were ambitious and they were keen,' she says. 'Eric was always a perfectionist. He wanted to be top class.'

Eric showed the same resolve when it came to courting Joan. After a week in Edinburgh they went their separate ways, but every Saturday night, after his last show, he'd catch the last train to wherever she was playing and spend a Sunday with her before travelling on to wherever he was playing next. 'He'd set his heart on the fact that I was going to be his girl, and that I was going to marry him. He was very determined. A lot of people would have given up.' He had a bit of luck as well. Three times, Eric and Joan were booked to play the same theatres, and then the boys got a gig in Margate, where Joan's mum and dad ran a seafront hotel. 'My mum will put you up,' said Joan. The same week Joan got a gig in Morecambe. 'You must go and stay with my mother,' said Eric. 'She'd love to have you.' And she did.

It was during this cross-country courtship that Eric and Ernie got their first gig at the London Palladium, the place every Variety act dreamt of playing, supporting their old friend 'Two Ton' Tessie O'Shea. It was a one-off broadcast for Radio Luxembourg rather than a week of twice-nightly, so for the first time in months, they actually had a few days free. And so, over the phone, Eric and Joan decided to get married. 'We'd only known each other a few months. It was very reckless, really.' But it was very romantic, too. They were married on 11 December 1952, at St John's in Margate. Joan had persuaded the vicar to marry them on a Sunday – Eric was working on Saturday. They travelled back to London and booked into the Cumberland Hotel, but they spent much of their wedding night going over Eric's lines for the Palladium show the next evening. Thanks to Joan's tuition, Eric remembered all his lines the next day, but there was still no time for a honeymoon. Instead the happy couple went straight up to Sheffield, where the boys were booked to play the Captain and his Mate in *Dick Whittington* at the Lyceum.

CHAPTER 16

ALAN CURTIS

ERIC AND JOAN HAD A TOUGH START to their married life. Soon after they arrived in Sheffield, Joan discovered that she was pregnant. 'It was very hard,' she says. 'We'd never intended that I should fall pregnant so soon, and that was hard because we didn't know each other terribly well. And Sheffield then wasn't like Sheffield is today. Sheffield then had all the smog. We had a very hard winter, with snow on the ground, I had terrible morning sickness, and the digs we went to, straight from being married, were absolutely dreadful.' They moved out and found a bedsit and things picked up a bit, but there was no central heating, and the pollution was so bad that Joan took to spending weekends in Morecambe with Eric's mum and dad. 'I was never, ever sick in Morecambe,' she says. 'And then I'd go back and start the sickness again, because they had all the smog and dirt and grime.'

*   *   *

Alan (second left) poses with, among others, Stan Stennett and Eric next to him, and Ernie with Doreen (far right).

Ernie and Doreen were married a month after Eric and Joan, on Sunday 18 January 1953 at the Baptist Chapel in Peterborough. Doreen had been running her own dancing school, and her pupils formed a guard of honour for the happy couple, their tap shoes held aloft. 'We had to get Eric married otherwise we'd have never been able to marry,' joshes Doreen. 'It would have been like Princess Diana! There would have been three in our marriage! We had to get rid of him!' Like Eric and Joan, they had no time for a honeymoon. They caught the train straight back up to Sheffield, in time for the Monday matinée. The star of the show was Ken Platt, still fondly remembered for his famous catchphrase, 'Hello, I won't take my coat off, I'm not stopping.' Ernie had booked a box for Doreen, and Eric kept looking up at her and grinning, which made her blush something rotten. 'Had it happened a few years later he would probably have stopped the show and announced the event to the audience, and made a big fuss about it, and got a wonderful reaction. But in those days Morecambe & Wise knew their place.'[1]

Ernie and Doreen's accommodation was even more basic than Joan and Eric's. In a bid to cut their travelling costs, Eric and Ernie had bought an old army truck for £125 from a builder in Llanelli, but it was prone to break-downs and collisions with fast-moving privet hedges, so they swapped it for an old bus that had been converted into a caravan. They planned to sleep in it while they were on tour, and save money on board and lodging, but it proved to be just as unreliable as the army truck, so they left it in Peterborough. Now Ernie and Doreen went and fetched it, and drove it back to Sheffield. It broke down en route, but they eventually made it to a garage in Lodge Moor, just outside Sheffield, on the edge of the Peak District. It wouldn't start again, so it stayed right there in the garage car park, and Ernie and Doreen stayed in it with only a paraffin heater (and each other) for warmth.

The Peak District is beautiful in summertime, but in winter it's a forbidding place, with winds that blow straight in from Siberia, or so the locals say. That winter was especially bleak. To reach their makeshift home, Ernie and Doreen had to clamber over snowdrifts more than six feet high, but they were young and newly wed and hopelessly in love, and they both remembered this ordeal with affection. 'I have fond memories of cosy evenings together with steaming mugs of tea after the evening show was over,' recalled Ernie, some forty years later. 'We have been inseparable ever since.'[2]

The working week was just as tough. For several months, they barely breathed a whiff of fresh air or saw a ray of sunshine. On matinée days they were in the theatre from before noon until after midnight, holed up in a poky dressing-room, their only refuge between shows. Joan and Doreen made this bolthole as cosy as they could but there was nothing glamorous about it. As Eric said, 'No matter how well you know a pantomime, it can be a pretty tiring way to earn a living.'[3] After rehearsing in unheated halls, half the cast were often suffering from colds and flu. Ernie usually had sinus trouble and frequently went on full of cures and potions. 'You've got to make a lot of laughs and a lot of fun in order to get through it all,' says Joan. 'You can't just do your lines.' It was their job to fill the theatre full of fun and laughter, but there was a darker side to panto that the punters never saw. Tony Heaton, who played the Dame, died in 1965 after walking into the sea at Blackpool. As Eric and Ernie knew all too well, being a comic could be a hard, hard life.

* * *

Dame Flora Robson as Queen Elizabeth I, Alan Curtis as King Philip of Spain, Eric Morecambe as William Shakespeare and Ernie Wise as Sir Walter Raleigh, BBC, 1971. Eric could never resist doing his impression of Long John Silver, whether at home or on screen.

Despite all their toil and trouble in Sheffield that long winter, the boys were a big hit in *Dick Whittington*, and a year later, at the end of 1953, they were invited back to the Lyceum to play third top in *Babes In The Wood*. Top of the bill was Freddie Sales, a super comic whose party piece was playing a baby in a playpen. Second top was Eric and Ernie's lifelong friend Stan Stennett, who was with Eric thirty years later, on the night he died. But although stars like Sales and Stennett drew the crowds, it was always the supporting players that held a really good pantomime together, and the boys were lucky to be cast alongside Alan Curtis, one of the great pantomime villains of the day. 'I didn't want to get laughs,' he says. 'I never tried to. I knew when you're working with a comic, let them get the laughs.'

Alan Curtis was born in 1930 and started work at the age of thirteen, making coffins and digging graves. 'I've had a bad back all my life,' he says. 'That definitely did it!' We're sitting in his home in Chiswick, not far from Mrs Duer's old boarding house, where Eric and Ernie used to live. Alan had been a keen amateur actor ever since he was a child, and at sixteen he got a job in Reigate, making puppet films for J. Arthur Rank. After that he painted the scenery for a summer season at Frinton-on-Sea, and in 1949, aged nineteen, he played his first pantomime, at the Penge Empire, helping the comics with their props and feeding them lines. For the next few years he worked all around the country, doing panto every Christmas and straight theatre throughout the year.

Weekly rep was a great training (there's nothing like it left today) but it was hard work. Alan was performing every evening and rehearsing next week's play every day. Between 1952 and 1953, he did seventy-two different plays in seventy-six weeks. 'I did actually have a few weeks out, when I didn't work in the evening, because otherwise it might have buried me.' And it wasn't all lightweight stuff. 'We gave the Scottish Play, *Macbeth*, and *The Merchant of Venice*, twice nightly.' On Tuesdays and Wednesdays they'd do two

Alan Curtis as Abanazar, Cliff Richard as Aladdin and Arthur Askey as Widow Twankey in *Aladdin*, Associated Rediffusion, 1967.

matinees — six Shakespeares in two days. It was after this theatrical marathon that he landed the role of the Sheriff in *Babes In The Wood* at the Sheffield Lyceum. The Robbers were Morecambe & Wise. 'I met them in the backstage canteen,' says Alan. 'We hit it off straight away.' He got on with both of them, but it was Eric who made the big impression. 'I immediately fell in awe of this man for whom everything was a gag. The speed and rapidity of the way he worked!'

Over fifty years later, Alan can still remember how much they were all paid. 'Freddie was getting £200, Stan was getting £150 and the boys were getting £120 between them,' says Alan. 'I was getting £30, which wasn't bad.' Not bad at all, when most working men earned less than a tenner. And even though Alan was on half their money, Eric and Ernie always treated him like an equal. They weren't big stars, just jobbing comics, and it wasn't in their nature to pull rank. They'd had enough hard knocks to know not to dish them out. Nice guys don't always finish last, and their fundamental decency played a big part in their eventual success. Audiences can sniff out insincerity and they soon tire of cynical comedians. They may laugh along the first few times, but they tend to only stick with acts they really like.

In 1954, Alan teamed up with Eric and Ernie again, in the same panto at the Derby Playhouse, and again at the Swansea Empire in 1955. 'You tended to put the cast together and try and keep it together to save money,' explains Alan. 'We weren't paid for rehearsal in those days. A good company would rehearse for a fortnight. Some of them would try and chuck it on in a week.' But there was no prospect of Eric and Ernie skimping on their preparation. Even their ad libs were honed and crafted to perfection. As Alan says, 'The job was absolutely the first thing in their lives.' Alan found out how serious they were about comedy, when he tried to borrow one of their precious joke books, which they guarded with their lives. 'No, you can't have that,' they said. 'I'm just going to look at it overnight,' said Alan. 'No!' they said, as they dragged him to the ground and wrestled it from his grasp.

Thankfully there were no hard feelings, and they all became firm friends. When they weren't working Alan would go for a spin in Ernie's car or join Eric at the movies. Eric invited him to his flat in Finchley, and Ernie

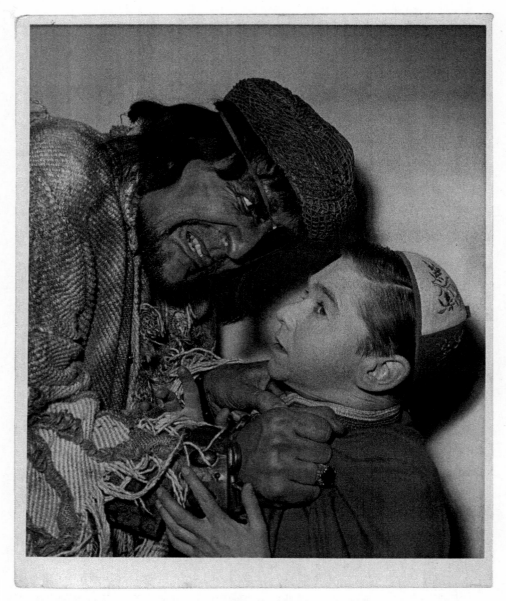

Alan Curtis as Abanazar and Jimmy Clitheroe as Wishee Washee in *Aladdin*, Grand Theatre Leeds, 1960–61.

and Doreen took him back to their house in Peterborough for Christmas. In the course of their long friendship, Alan gained a unique insight into the workings of Britain's greatest double act, including the remarkable revelation that their biggest inspiration wasn't a British double act like Jewel and Warriss, but an American duo called Wheeler and Woolsey. This vaudeville duo are almost forgotten now, but when Eric and Ernie were just starting out they were at the peak of their careers. During the 1930s they made more than twenty movies, making more money for their studio, RKO, than any of RKO's other stars. Woolsey wore round horn-rimmed glasses, just like Eric in his early days, and from a distance the resemblance is remarkable. There was another similarity as well, although Eric and Ernie would have been oblivious to it at the time. The straight man, Bert Wheeler, lived to a grand old age, like Ernie. Like Eric, the comic, Robert Woolsey, died too young.

The last time Alan worked with them in pantomime was in *Dick Whittington* in 1956 at the Dudley Hippodrome, alongside the Canadian close harmony quartet, The Maple Leaf Four. Stan Stennett was in the show again, but the biggest draw was the female impersonator Rex Coster, aka Mrs Shufflewick. Coster had started off playing a comic vicar at the Windmill Theatre and created Mrs Shufflewick because his vicar was too lewd for radio. Roy Hudd describes her best. 'She was the woman down the pub who, outwardly fairly prim, would suddenly spill out tales of sexual adventures that would make your hair curl.'[4] 'He had this marvellous reputation in the London clubs,' says Alan. 'He became a sort of gay cult.' He gave Alan a signed photo. On it he'd written, 'My darling, I hope I'll be your leading lady sometime!'

After they stopped doing pantomime together, Alan and the boys still kept in touch, and he ended up working with them on TV. He used to catch their live act as often as he could ('Eric was a terrific worrier – I used to go and see him before the show but I never stayed very long') but he's sad that so many of the theatres where they played have been torn down to make way for car parks, supermarkets and shopping centres. 'They should have hung on to these theatres,' he says. 'They sold the buildings the moment they saw which way the wind was blowing.' Luckily, Eric and Ernie got out just in time.

CHAPTER 17

STAN STENNETT

SADLY, STAN STENNETT is probably most familiar to younger Morecambe
& Wise fans as the man who was with Eric on the night he died, in 1984.
However there's far more to Stan than that final curtain call. The reason he
was onstage with Eric that final evening, at the Roses Theatre in Tewkesbury,
was because he'd had so much to do with Eric and Ernie through the years, as
a colleague and a friend. In particular, he appeared with them in panto, a
crucial stage in their development as a double act, and although Stan was born
in the same year as Ernie, he was still appearing in pantomime last Christmas.
It was his sixtieth year in panto. He was eighty-one years old.

*   *   *

Above **Eric and Ernie either side of Stan Stennett. The boys would often appear on Stan's summer season and pantos during the fifties.**

Opposite **'Now, now boys!' Says the great pantomime Dame, Rex Holdsworth (second left). Stan Stennett (left) and Morecambe & Wise (right) listen in.** *Babes in the Wood*, Derby Playhouse, 1954–55.

Stan Stennett was born in 1925 in Bridgend, not far from Cardiff, and began his showbiz career in his early teens, playing the guitar with local jazz groups in working men's clubs. He was called up in 1943, served in the artillery during the Second World War and appeared in the forces revue, *Stars In Battledress*. He came out of the army in 1947 and went back to his old day job, working for Pickfords, the furniture removal people, but he kept gigging in the evenings, and after winning a local talent contest, he was spotted by the producer of a radio show called *Welsh Rarebit*. Stan became one of the two resident comics. The other was Harry Secombe. He formed a comical musical trio called the Harmaniacs, and joined Max Miller's live show, playing theatres like the Chiswick Empire, the Hackney Empire, the Shepherd's Bush Empire and that grand old music hall, the Metropolitan Edgware Road. 'Max didn't like to work too far outside London, being a Brighton boy,' says Stan, recalling his apprenticeship playing twice nightly with the legendary Cheekie Chappie, who always stayed just the right side of blue. 'He'd finish the first show as the top of the bill, but in the second show he'd finish the first half, so he could get his train back to Brighton.' For Stan, it was the ideal introduction to the world

Above **Eric (right) and his wife Joan (left) with Stan Stennett and his wife Betty (centre).**

Below **Stan Stennett at the wheel, Eric and Ernie in the passenger seat and the ladies keep the boot closed.**

of live Variety. 'Max was the perfect stand-up comic. Wherever he went, Max was adored.'

In 1951 Stan went solo. By 1953 he was playing the London Palladium, the dream of every Light Ent turn. Billed as 'certified insanely funny', his act was a mad amalgam of music, one-liners and impressions. 'We always looked forward to Stan coming to our local,' recalled Roy Hudd.[1] He wasn't the only one. Stan worked with Bob Hope and Johnny Ray. He even went down well at the Glasgow Empire. And in Christmas 1953 he was booked to play Silly Billy in *Babes In The Wood* at the Lyceum Theatre in Sheffield. The Robbers were a jobbing double act called Morecambe & Wise.

Stan had never seen Eric and Ernie's act before, but he bonded with them from day one. 'On the day we first met for rehearsal, we did nothing but tell each other gags.' Pantomimes depend on this sort of chemistry. No wonder the write ups were fantastic. 'There was so much ad-libbing in the show,' he says. 'We'd set each other off.' They had just as much fun doing *Babes In The Wood* at the Derby Playhouse in 1954 and the Swansea Empire in 1955, and *Dick Whittington* at the Dudley Hippodrome in 1956. Stan played Idle Jack. Eric and Ernie played the Captain and his Mate.

As well as the running gags onstage, there were also lots of jokes backstage. There was a celebrated scene in *Dick Whittington* called The Rocking Cabin, which created the illusion of a storm at sea. The cabin was on rockers, and beneath it was a tank containing thousands of gallons of water, which would pour in through the portholes as the cabin rocked from side to side. 'Twice daily I got drowned, practically,' says Stan. 'In would come a wall of water.' Thankfully, the water was heated, or at least it would have been if Eric hadn't intervened. 'Eric went round sabotaging it, so they didn't heat it, so I got bloody cold!' says Stan, with a chuckle. 'It was him! He'd done something to the heating! He was a real joker!'

That wasn't Eric's only prank. 'I used to have a couple of love scenes with the principal girl. He would get behind the backcloth with a Whoopee cushion under his arm, making all sorts of bloody rude noises!' In those patriotic days, the cast would still finish off by singing the national anthem. Eric would hide the Whoopee cushion under his cloak. The audience couldn't hear a thing but the cast could hardly contain themselves. 'We should have all been put in the bloody Tower of London!' says Stan.

The Derby Hippodrome, with star billing for Stan Stennet (third left), Eric (third right) and Ernie (second right) in the 1954 production of *Babes in the Wood*.

134

CHAPTER 18

BLACKPOOL

'THEY WERE SECOND TOP OF THE BILL for a long time,' remembers Joan. 'Eric was quite happy to be second top, because you had some sort of position in showbusiness, and you never stopped working. You were very lucky to always be working in showbusiness. You were privileged to be in work. But you didn't carry the responsibility that you did as top of the bill. If the bookings were bad, or it didn't go well, the poor old top of the bill always took the blame. They had to be the one that drew the people in.'

Most acts dreamt of being top of the bill, but years of hard grind had taught Eric and Ernie to be more cautious. Playing second top, they were free from the critical and commercial pressure that always plagues a headline act. It wasn't down to them how many tickets were sold or what the reviews were like. 'Second tops are better,' Ernie used to tell Eric. 'Let's just stick to being

a good, reliable act. It's safer.'[1] And Eric agreed. 'Once you have topped bills, it's hard – not just to step down on a bill but even to get work.'[2] Acts like Wilson, Keppel and Betty were making £100 a week – a substantial sum in 1950, when the average weekly wage was less than £10. Their routine never varied, they never topped the bill, yet they were never out of work. Over the course of their long careers, they made far more money than those headline acts who topped the bill for a few years, then fell out of favour.

Playing a new town and a new venue every week allowed Eric and Ernie to refine their act in relative anonymity. 'With television came all the stress and strain,' says Joan. 'With Variety, you did the same act week after week. Eric and Ernie were very good at trying to put in new bits of material, but you still did the same act week after week. You got your living from that. The old showbusiness people, they'd expect to do a whole lifetime of the same material.' Eric and Ernie were far too bright (and far too ambitious) for that,

Above **A long-suffering Gail and Gary wait while their Dad and Ernie pose with a holidaymaker.**
Opposite **Eric and Ernie on Blackpool beach, promoting the local oysters in front of the famous tower.**

137

but this weekly live routine enabled them to develop at their own pace. New material was now a bonus, not a necessity, so they could work on building their stage rapport rather than learning reams of jokes.

By now they were able to really work the room, bouncing topical gags off the audience and even other acts. One time, they were asked to do a few extra minutes, to fill in for zither player Anton Karas. Karas had suddenly become an international star on the back of Carol Reed's subterranean film noir, *The Third Man*, in which he played the theme tune, but there wasn't much else to his act, and his set usually fell some way short of his allotted ten minutes. Eric solved the problem by coming on with his coat collar turned up, like Orson Welles in the movie. 'I've just come out of a sewer,' he told Ernie. 'There's this fella playing a boring tune on a broken piano.'[3]

Playing a different town every week was fine if you were single, but since Eric and Ernie were both married, they always looked forward to summer season, when they'd be booked for an entire summer in the same show, in the same seaside resort. As Doreen says, 'You could have a normal married life there because you rented a house, so you could take all your pots and pans.' And the acts saw a lot more of each other, too. 'It's only when you do a season, in either summer season or pantomime, that you have time together,' says Joan. 'Particularly with comics, there's always a lot of laughs.'

The booking all Variety entertainers yearned to get was a Summer Season in Blackpool, and in 1953 Eric and finally Ernie got it. The producers were Alfred Black and his brother George, who'd hired them for *Strike A New Note*. 'You are going to do well, we know it,' Alfred told them. 'Now go out there and hit them between the eyes.'[4] In those days, Blackpool summer season ran from April right through until October, and the frequently filthy weather meant that there was a big demand for indoor entertainment. Punters would come out of a show and book the same seats for the same night the following year. Back then, Blackpool boasted eleven different theatres: the Opera House, the Blackpool Tower, the North, South and Central Piers, Feldman's Theatre, the Grand Theatre, the Queen's Theatre, the Palace Theatre and the Hippodrome, plus the Winter Gardens, where the boys were booked to play, alongside Yorkshire comedian Harry Worth, Lancashire comic Ken Platt and Welsh singer Alan Jones (the Queen's, the Palace and the Hippodrome are all long gone, but the rest are all still there).

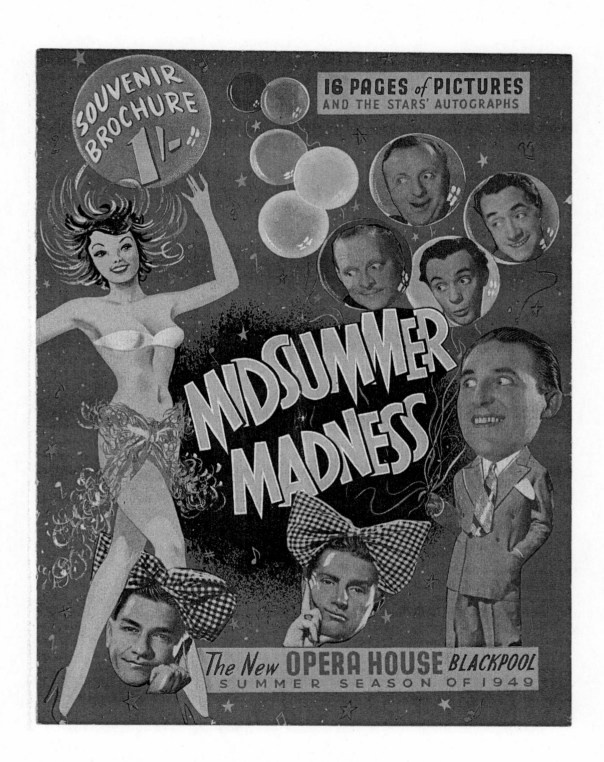

Sheila Mathews beat Eric and Ernie to Blackpool, landing the coveted summer season spot four years before them, in 1949.

"Out of this World" ARTISTES from all over the World

TESSIE O'SHEA
"Blackpools Own"

NAT JACKLEY
from Sunderland

...RY DESMONDE
...Middlesbrough

THE PREMIER VARIETY JOURNAL

THE PERFORMER

THE OFFICIAL ORGAN OF THE VARIETY ARTISTES' FEDERATION

DAVY KAYE
"Wishee Washee"
Will Collins'
PANTOMIME
EMPIRE,
SHEPHERD'S BUSH
WILL COLLINS

BILLY WHITTAKER AND MIMI LAW
"WINDMILL FOLLIES"
Direction: JACK ADAMS

Vol. XCV No. 2428   THURSDAY, DECEMBER 4, 1952.   Price 6d.

FRANK POPE   NATIONAL THEATRICAL VARIETY AGENCY
Gen. Manager: WILLIAM SULLIVAN

Exclusively Representing

F. J. B. THEATRES LTD.

(Managing Director: F. J. BUTTERWORTH, Esq.)

HIPPODROME · WOLVERHAMPTON   EMPIRE · YORK   BRISTOL
HIPPODROME · BOURNEMOUTH   EMPIRE · GRIMSBY
HIPPODROME · ASTON   PALACE   LINCOLN
HIPPODROME · NORWICH   THEATRE ROYAL   SCUNTHORPE
GRAND · SOUTHAMPTON   SAVOY

— also —

THOSE UP AND COMING STARS

ERIC   ERNIE
MORECAMBE & WISE

FULLY BOOKED FOR 1953 with

GEORGE and ALFRED BLACK LTD.

INCLUDING SUMMER SEASON AT THE PAVILION THEATRE, BLACKPOOL

[They extend their thanks to LEW & LESLIE GRADE LTD. for a year's happy engagement]

— also —

RALPH BARBER & F. J. BUTTERWORTH

(PRODUCTIONS) LTD.

TERRY-THOMAS
from London

GLORIA WILLIAMS
from Australia

...IVE OLANDERS
...Denmark

SHEILA MATHEWS
from London

Left Frank Pope was sole agent for Morecambe & Wise in their early days and was responsible for getting their Variety dates. They finally, and reluctantly, went their separate ways when Eric and Ernie realized they needed a bigger agent to get them on to television.

Eric's old West End dancing partner, Sheila Mathews, had also gone on to star in shows at Blackpool. 'There were thirteen live shows in Blackpool in the summer,' she says. 'It was incredible. Jewel and Warriss were on the North Pier, Dave Morris was at the Grand, Sid Field was at the Opera House. It was unbelievable.' No wonder people called it Lancashire's answer to Las Vegas. 'Cars couldn't drive down the road there were so many crowds. We used to be there from the end of May until October, and then I'd go straight into pantomime after that, which used to last into April.' She played the Opera House three years running, first with Charlie Chester, then with Nat 'Rubberneck' Jackley and 'Two Ton' Tessie O'Shea. When Tessie was rushed into hospital with appendicitis, Sheila had to stand in for her. You can hardly imagine a more unlikely understudy. Tessie was enormous, Sheila was a slip of a thing, but she was the only one who knew all the songs, and like a proper trooper, she carried it off. So what made it so different from all the other resorts? 'It was bigger, larger, louder, noisier, gayer and certainly brighter. It had a wonderful festive feeling about it. The shops were marvellous, and all those theatres — everybody out to have a damn good time.'

Like many British seaside towns, Blackpool was a product of the Industrial Revolution, but nowhere took off quite as quickly as this windswept resort. It was the nearest stretch of beach to all those Lancastrian mill towns, back in the bad old days when mill workers worked six days a week, and needed a resort that was near enough for day trips, close enough to travel to in time for church

Ernie with friends and family on the Blackpool seafront.

on Sunday morning. When the mill owners were finally forced to give their workers a week's annual holiday, each mill town took it in turns to shut up shop and come to Blackpool for a week. Blackpool wasn't founded in the eighteenth century, as an aristocratic spa town, like Brighton. It was founded in the nineteenth century, for the amusement of the working class.

The thing that really changed Blackpool was the railway. In 1841, Blackpool's population was still only 2000. The railway arrived in 1846, and by 1860 its population had doubled. In 1863, 20,000 people travelled there by train for the opening of Blackpool's North Pier. The Central Pier opened five years later, and in 1871, the Bank Holiday Act brought even greater numbers to the seaside. The electric trams arrived in 1885, followed in 1894 by the Tower and the Grand Theatre, built by Variety's greatest architect, Frank Matcham. Unlike a lot of other seaside towns, Blackpool welcomed the working classes, rather than trying to discourage them, and by 1900 it had become Britain's leading resort, with two million visitors every year.

There were sixty ice cream stalls along the front and forty oyster stalls. At one time, holidaymakers here were getting through three quarters of a million oysters every week, which must have done wonders for their sex drive.

In the roof gardens beneath the Tower lived a troupe of forty midgets. Some of them worked at the Pleasure Beach, driving steam trains on the miniature railway. The lifeboat station was the only one in Britain with its own brass band. Blackpool peaked between the wars but in 1953 it was still booming, and the seven-mile promenade was swarming with visitors, over a million at any one time. As Eric used to say, 'If a gull was flying overhead and actually tried to miss somebody it would have been a miraculous feat.'[5]

Eric was a keen football fan (he'd been a decent player as a lad) and when he was in Blackpool he used to go along to Bloomfield Road to watch Britain's greatest footballer, Sir Stanley Matthews. When Blackpool bought Matthews from Stoke City in 1947, he was already in his early thirties, an age when most wingers start thinking about hanging up their boots, yet 'the Wizard of the Dribble' kept on playing until he was fifty, and when Eric and Ernie came to Blackpool in 1953, he'd just won the FA Cup for them, more or less single-handed, in what most anoraks rightly regard as the greatest cup final of all time.

*   *   *

Eric's first Blackpool summer season was rudely interrupted by the birth of his first child, at his parents' house in Morecambe, on 13 September 1953. 'We rented a house in Blackpool first of all, and then when it got nearer the time to have the baby we lived in Morecambe,' says Joan. 'By then Eric had passed his driving test and that was his practice run, backwards and forwards from Morecambe to Blackpool.' Joan went into labour on a Sunday morning, but it was a terribly difficult birth and she was still in labour on the Monday afternoon. Eric had to set off in good time, since the theatre was nearly thirty miles away. 'He had to leave to go to work with me still not having had the baby,' says Joan. 'He was such a nervous wreck.' And no wonder. Imagine having to go out on a night like that and entertain a bunch of strangers.

The boys were halfway through their opening routine when Eric spotted the conductor gesticulating wildly in the orchestra pit. 'It's a girl!' he mouthed. When the boys came off after their first spot, the stage manager confirmed the news. Joan had given birth to a six-pound baby girl. Eric got

permission to leave the theatre before the finale, and Alan Jones, who was somewhat partial to an occasional drop of liquid refreshment, explained Eric's absence to the audience. 'You'll notice that Eric Morecambe was not with us for the finale,' he announced. 'He's rushing home this very minute to his wife because he has just become the father of a six-month baby girl.'[6]

As Ernie put it, with his usual tact, the sea air didn't really agree with Alan, and he'd sometimes retire with a large bottle of something potent by way of compensation. Consequently, recollected Ernie, he would occasionally fail to appear onstage. George and Alfred Black were mindful of this possibility, and told Eric and Ernie to be ready to fill in for him if the need arose. It was quite a compliment to be asked to deputize for a headliner, but the boys were anything but pleased. They'd used up all their material in their two supporting slots. They didn't have anything left over for a closing routine.

Sure enough, Eric and Ernie were in their dressing-room one night after their second spot, listening to Alan's performance, when they heard his voice start to crack. The next thing they heard was the sound of running footsteps. It was George Black, running along the corridor, to tell them to take over. Quick as a flash, the boys took off all their clothes. 'We aren't anywhere near ready,' they told him, when he burst in. 'You'd better get someone else.' Thankfully, this rather transparent ruse didn't hold them back. They went back to Blackpool for four more summer seasons, at the Central Pier in 1955, 1957 and 1959, and the North Pier in 1963. 'They were using a sketch in which Eric interrupted Ernie's attempts to sing by crunching mouthfuls of potato crisps into the microphone,' recalls Blackpool author Barry Band, who interviewed the boys backstage at the Central Pier in 1959, while working as a reporter for the local paper. 'Their dressing-room was stacked with boxes of crisps, and Eric must have eaten four packets a night for eighteen weeks. I have often wondered if his intake of salty, fatty crisps contributed to his poor health.'

Above **The mayor of Morecambe poses with his illustrious guests, including Eric and Ernie and Alma Cogan.**

Above **Attending beauty pageants went with the territory when you did summer season. With Eric and Ernie is their friend, Alma Cogan, who died tragically young, of cancer, aged just 34.**

CHAPTER 19

GAIL MORECAMBE

IT WAS A BLESSING that Gail was born while Eric was in Blackpool, but a month later the season ended, and the boys were back on the road. And as Eric soon discovered, touring with a newborn baby was no joke. 'It was terribly hard,' says Joan. 'It's a wonder really that any marriage stands up to it.' They were travelling every weekend, living out of suitcases, trekking from town to town on public transport, often in filthy weather. 'You never had a free day,' she says. 'You'd do these hellish long journeys.' It was tough enough when it was just the two of them, but now they had Gail to look after too. They couldn't afford hotels, and the guest houses they stayed in were hardly ideal for a baby. They were all cooped up in one room, with Gail in a carry-cot at the foot of the bed. There were no disposable nappies in those days, so Joan had to wash them all by hand. 'You've got no central heating. You've not

MY FAVOURITE'S

Above **Two of Eric's favourite photographs of his daughter Gail.**
Opposite **Gail enjoys a game with her granddad.**

necessarily got a lot of running hot water. Some of the digs were lovely. I don't want to run them all down. But an awful lot were very mediocre.'

You could say that again. 'I remember a really crummy joint in Wigan,' recalled Eric, at the peak of his career. 'When we got up in the morning, Joan's face was blotched and swollen, and the baby's face was so swollen you could barely see her eyes.'[1] Eric pulled back the bed covers. The bed was full of bed bugs. He marched downstairs to remonstrate with the landlady. 'We're leaving this filthy place,' he told her. 'It's riddled with bedbugs!' 'Yes, leave,' she said, 'and take your filthy bedbugs with you!'[2] It was January 1954, a cold winter's day in Lancashire. Gail was just four months old.

When Gail was three, Joan gave birth to Gary, which made things even tougher. Touring with one child was hard, touring with two was impossible, but luckily by now Eric and Ernie were making a bit more money, so when Gary was three Eric bought a house in Finchley, which made life much easier. Practical as ever, Joan converted the house into two flats. They lived in one

151

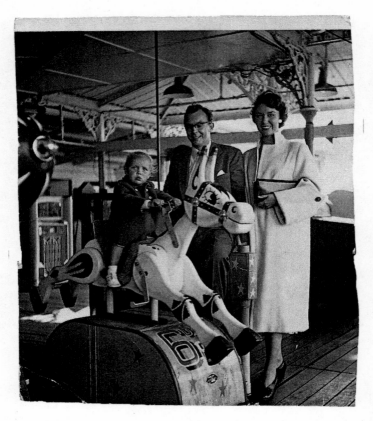

Eric and Joan encouraging Gail to like horses. It must have worked – she ended up with two of them, and didn't stop riding until in her forties, when allergies finally got the better of her.

and rented out the other. However, Eric was still touring, so he saw a lot less of his family. 'In our very early years he wasn't around all that much,' says Gail. We're sitting in the kitchen of her country home, a converted school-house. She's got her mother's slender figure, but her face is all her father's — the same pointed nose, the same sharp eyes, the same shy but impish grin.

'Every summer when school broke up, we'd rent a house wherever dad was doing summer season,' she says. 'We'd rent a seaside bungalow, and we'd spend the entire eight weeks at the seaside.' Gail is in her early fifties now, but her eyes still light up when she talks about it. 'For a child, it was just magical. Somehow, every day in my memory it's summer.'

In the mornings, Eric would take Gail to the theatre to collect his post. They'd go in through the stage door and sit together in his dressing-room while he went through his mail. This simple chore was one of her favourite routines. There were often friends or relatives at the house, and everywhere else he was surrounded by strangers. This was her special time alone with him. In the evenings, after Eric had gone to work, her mum would take her and Gary for a walk along the seafront. One of the perks of Eric's job was that he'd be given books of tickets for the fairground, so they'd go on all the rides for free. Gail was mad about horses, so she loved the carousels.

By the time Gail was ten she'd become very keen on real horses, so wherever her dad was playing summer season she'd find a local stable where she could ride. Every day she'd be at the stables, mucking out the horses and cleaning up the yard. At Yarmouth, the horses in the yard where she got a summer job were working on the seafront, so she'd ride them from the stables across the fields and dunes to the shore.

Because she was so small, the theatres all seemed huge. She loved the sight, the sound, the smell of them. It was thrilling to go backstage, where the public never ventured. Eric and Ernie's dressing-room was always full of people, but her dad made sure she never became infatuated with his career. The only time she ever saw him lose his temper was when she wandered into the dancing girls' dressing-room, and they made her up like a showgirl. Eric got really upset. Gail was only four, but she got the message. This wasn't the place

for a nice girl. 'If I'd wanted to be an opera singer it probably would have been all right, but he didn't really want me in showbusiness.' There wasn't much danger of that. Up close, behind the scenes, she could see the false eyelashes, the thick make-up, the sweat and toil. 'You're seeing what's behind the illusion,' she says. 'It wasn't a glamorous business to be in.'

However Eric was happy to let her watch him work. 'Every now and then I'd be allowed to go by myself to actually watch a performance. Those were the moments when I'd be completely filled with pride. One of the things I liked was sitting there knowing that he was my father and that nobody around me knew that, and I enjoyed that. I didn't have any urge to turn to anyone and say, "That's my daddy." It was like my little secret.' And then her dad and Ernie would come out and work their magic. 'I could actually just sit and watch the person next to me because it was so enthralling,' she says. 'That power, that gift of making people belly-laugh, so that the tears were streaming down their faces! I really loved that. That was huge.'

It was all the other offstage stuff she wasn't quite so keen on. 'Not being able to go on the beach with dad, not being able to just walk into a café, because people felt they knew him.' Eric realized he needed fame to bolster his career, but unlike a lot of stars, he didn't need it to bolster his feelings of self-worth. 'He profoundly understood the meaninglessness of fame. He knew that it was everything and nothing.' More than any other comic, it was his special gift to create that aura of familiarity, but this meant his family had to share him with the millions of strangers who believed in that illusion. 'He always had time for them. He would never say, "I don't want to do this now — I'm out with my family."' And inevitably, Gail wasn't quite sure how to respond. 'Part of me thought it was wonderful that people talked to him and would call his name, but another part of me would find it very intrusive.'

Compared to the lavish showbiz lifestyles you read about nowadays, Eric and Ernie lived very simply. When they did a season in Weymouth, they spent the summer in a couple of rented caravans on a local caravan site. Gail and Gary had a great time, but Joan found it hard going. Their family caravan was even smaller than Ernie and Doreen's, and it wasn't even en suite. The nearest toilet was a walk away, at the bottom of the hill.

When Eric was working in the north of England, his family would stay with Eric's parents. When they were working in the south, they'd stay with Joan's mum and dad. Even when they started making decent money, Eric and Ernie both preferred saving to spending. Ernie was naturally careful, and Eric was always worried about providing for his children. After struggling for so long to become successful, they never knew how long it would last.

When Eric and Ernie's first TV series, *Running Wild*, was lambasted by the critics, Eric cut out the most damning review ('Definition of the week — TV set: the box in which they buried Morecambe & Wise') and carried it in his wallet until the day he died. 'He didn't carry it around with him because it hurt him so much,' says Gail. 'He carried it around with him as a little reminder, that you could get an article like that the next day, that it was very fickle. You could be the greatest thing one day and gone the next.'

Eric was similarly sanguine when reporters wrote nasty or inaccurate things about Gail. 'It's tomorrow's fish and chip paper,' he used to tell her. 'If you believe the good things that people write about you then you have to believe the bad things as well, so it's best not to believe either because there's as much and as little truth in both.' Yet although she cherished those times at home with him, in a way he was always on. 'He had to leave you laughing,' she says. 'As he'd walk out of the room and disappear you'd hear him say, "You'll miss me. You'll miss me when I'm gone."'

Above **Eric and the women in his life: his mother Sadie and wife Joan.**

Below **A rare shot of both the Wises with all the Morecambes, at the opening of a summer fete.**

Two rare publicity shots of Eric and Ernie with Northern comic legend, Jimmy Clitheroe. The diminutive Clitheroe specialized in playing a schoolboy. When these photographs were taken he was a bigger star than Morecambe & Wise.

CHAPTER 20

GARY MORECAMBE

BY THE TIME GARY MORECAMBE WAS BORN, in 1956, three years after Gail, Eric and Ernie had clawed their way back from the failure of their first TV series, *Running Wild*, to become regular guest stars on TV. However it would still be five more years before they were given another series of their own, and in the meantime live comedy remained their regular bread and butter.

With a wife and two children to support, Eric hated to turn down any paid work, and the demands of TV, radio and Variety left him little time at home. Since Eric's death, Gary Morecambe has done more than anyone to preserve his father's reputation, publishing several books about Morecambe & Wise and collaborating with numerous documentary-makers, but this work has been tinged with sadness, an attempt to make the most of a relationship

Doreen and the kids enjoy a moment outside in the sunshine.

that was warm, but far too fleeting. When Gary was a boy, Eric was often away working. During the family's first year in their new home in Harpenden, Eric spent only twenty nights at home. After Eric's first heart attack, in 1968, he cut back his live commitments, and started living a life that was a bit more nine-to-five. However by this time Gary was away at boarding school. It was during the school holidays that he really got a chance to see his dad, especially the summer holidays, when Eric was doing summer season.

'That's the strange thing,' says Gary, over a cup of coffee in his flat in Bristol. 'Most of my memories always come from Morecambe & Wise, really, whereas Gail's all come from him being dad. My earliest memory of him is realizing who he was – realizing he was Eric Morecambe, the comedian, which is when I was five. I was aware of that because that year, at the age of five, was when I started at primary school, and other people knew who my father was.' Gail's formative years were very different. When she started school, Eric and Ernie were only occasional guest stars on TV. They were only really famous in two towns every year, wherever they were doing pantomime and summer season. However when Gary started school, in 1961, Eric and Ernie had just started

their long-running show for Lew Grade's ATV. Gail had her father to herself, for the first few years at least. Gary never had the same sort of privacy. Right from the start, his dad was always a household name. 'I knew at the age of five my life would never be the same again.'

Summertime was a welcome break, a chance to swap the ubiquity of TV for the more intimate fame of summer season. 'As kids, we had long holidays, so we could easily be transported to the venues for six weeks at a time, which was wonderful,' recalls Gary. 'What I really liked was standing at the side of the stage and getting to see all the acts.' Gary would see the show almost every day, watching his dad at work while eating an ice cream in the wings. 'Eric and Ernie's spot was so sharp and slick, it wasn't that different from what you saw on TV in the later years,' he says. 'I was really proud. I got great pleasure out of watching that. It was so funny.' The chemistry between them was something that really struck him, but what impressed him most of all was how well they worked the room. 'They didn't go out there and just tell gags.' They were much more intimate. In an age when a comedian's job was to crack jokes, this was really quite revolutionary.

The other acts were all more traditional – musicians, acrobats, even midgets, which used to terrify Gary. 'There was something very scary about these little people running round.' During one of their Christmas pantomimes, Eric and Ernie shared a dressing room in the bowels of the theatre, and Gary used to ride the lift that carried them up from the basement to the stage. One time, he found himself in the lift with Eric and Ernie, and the actress who played the wicked witch, in full costume, her face caked in green make-up. 'Oh, you're a nice little boy!' she told him. Gary was absolutely petrified, but Eric and Ernie just laughed. 'All my friends had fathers who were lawyers or bankers. Here was my father, dressed in tights, in a lift with a witch.'

It was a side of showbusiness that most five-year-olds never see. 'What I realized as a kid, being backstage so much of the time, is that the whole thing is an illusion.' From the safety of the stalls, it all looked wonderful, but from the wings, he could see the sweat on the painted faces of the dancing girls, more like athletes than artistes in their thick, functional body stockings. 'From the other side of the footlights, they looked long legged and attractive. Close up, they had tree-trunk legs.' It was like being in the dugout at a football match. All the glamour had been stripped away.

'Although the Variety halls were closing, no one had told the inmates,' says Gary. 'They were still happily going out and doing their ridiculous, preposterous acts because they needed to make a crust. They didn't have bank accounts or credit cards in those days. They survived on what they earned, and they'd tour the whole land to achieve that. They couldn't escape it, even

Gary shares a loving moment with his granddad, Eric's father George.

Gary and Gail relax at home with their granny and granddad, Eric's parents, George and Sadie.

Opposite Eric and his son Gary on Morecambe FC's football pitch at Christie Park. Eric used to watch the team as a kid. How pleased he would have been to see them promoted to the Football League for the first time in their history, in 2007. Gary still keeps in contact with the club.

though they knew the ship was sinking, so they carried on as if nothing was happening, which in the end would destroy them anyway.'

Eric and Ernie were one of the few acts who actually moved with the times. 'They always kept changing,' says Gary. 'They always kept developing.' Alongside these antiquated turns, they seemed so modern, in their sharp suits, with their quick-fire patter. 'They were new and they were fresh,' says Gary. 'They acted like stars. They shone.' But Gary could see what a strain it was. 'I liked it, but it scared the hell out of me. You could see it was stressful work. I didn't want to do it. I knew that. It was great looking into the gold-fish bowl, but I didn't want to join the fish.' Sometimes, when they were waiting in the wings, Eric would grab Gary and threaten to drag him out onstage. 'Are you coming on with us?' he'd ask his son. Gary would be terri-fied. Eric would just laugh, let him go, and then walk out onto the stage.

And yet, despite his immense talent, Eric remained ambivalent about showbiz. Ernie was a born showman, but Eric was always in two minds about it. 'I don't think being a big star ever sat comfortably with Eric,' says Gary. 'I think there was a part of him that was like his father — that happy-go-lucky

streak, and had to fight that quite ferociously to keep his own enthusiasm going, the enthusiasm his mother had instilled. His mother used to say, "Without me, he'd have been bone idle," and I think that's probably true.'

Eric also had mixed feelings about fame. 'He'd come out for a walk with us, but he'd get recognized all the time.' If Eric had been a bit more brusque, he might have retained some privacy, but that wasn't in his nature. 'He never wanted to let anyone down, so he'd be Eric Morecambe for them all the time. In the process, of course, he was letting his family down. For Gail and me, it was a pain in the arse.' Eric's genius, and his curse, was that everyone felt they knew him. Like Gail, Gary found it hard to share his father with the world at large. 'He was only trying to do his job, and help sell tickets, and make a successful show for everyone, but sometimes he got a bit carried away.' When strangers approached them in the street, Eric would turn on the routine. 'We saw your show last night,' they used to say. 'Oh, are we still friends?' Eric would reply. Even if he was feeling stressed, he always had to put his public first. Gary used to wonder why on earth his dad would want to do this for a living. 'As Rowan Atkinson once said, living with Eric must have been hard for his family, but imagine living with Eric and being Eric.' Rowan visited Eric at his home in Harpenden, but he didn't meet Eric through showbusiness. He was actually a friend of a friend of Gary's.

Eric and Ernie were on their way up, most of the acts they worked with were on their way down, and Gary soon realized that both these destinations had their own hardships. Sooner or later, all star-struck kids find out that showbiz is a tough life, but Gary found out a lot sooner than most. 'Walking past the dressing rooms, I sometimes saw the ventriloquist's dummy, discarded on the dressing-room table like a dead body, eyes wide open, blank.' Even so, he saw some great acts from the wings, and even got to know them too. One of his favourites, onstage and offstage, was a funny fellow in a badly fitting bowler hat called Freddie 'Parrot Face' Davies. 'What I liked about him was that he was very gentle,' says Gary. 'He had such a lovely, gentle face — and he was just like that offstage as well. As a kid, I was very inhibited. I was very wary of all these stagey people, but he was one I really warmed to.'

Left **Eric, Ernie and a Scottish Highland Terrier. The dogs came and went but Ernie and Doreen stayed faithful to the breed.**

Below **The boys get ready for a spot of bowls.**

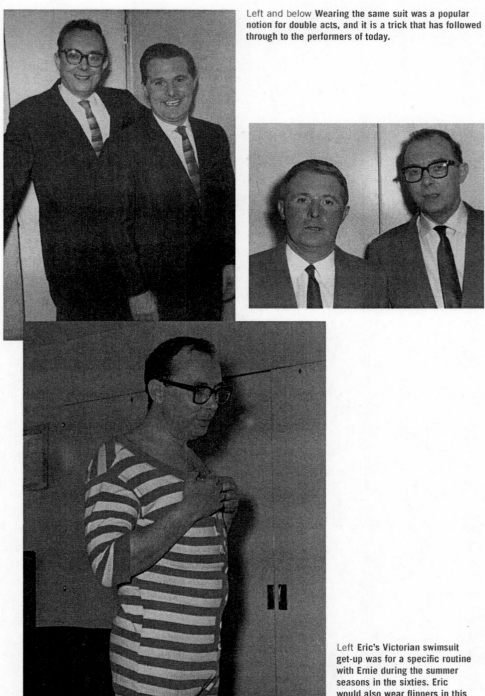

Left and below **Wearing the same suit was a popular notion for double acts, and it is a trick that has followed through to the performers of today.**

Left **Eric's Victorian swimsuit get-up was for a specific routine with Ernie during the summer seasons in the sixties. Eric would also wear flippers in this routine. By now they were topping the bill.**

Left **'You can't get out of that!'** is the suggestion made in this 1960s drawing by Chic. This saying and hand action by Eric pre-dates the more expedient attacks on Ernie with the slaps on the face.

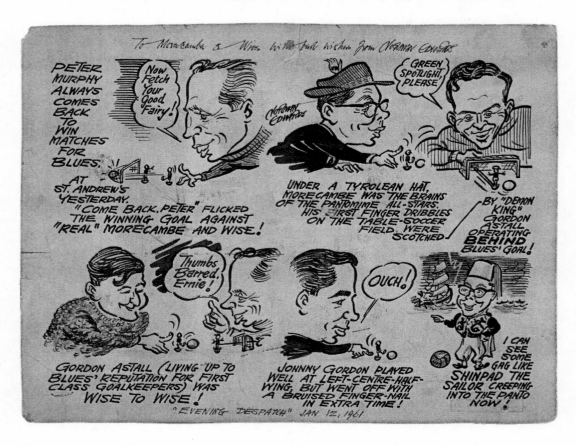

CHAPTER 21

FREDDIE DAVIES

FREDDIE DAVIES COMES FROM a proper showbusiness family. His mother was a dancer and both her parents were entertainers. They used to do a double act in the Variety halls between the wars. Born in 1937, Freddie is a bit too young to remember their heyday, but he saw them onstage several times, alongside all sorts of eccentric entertainers, like Tommy Toes Jacobson — a man with no arms who played the piano with his feet — and threw darts as well.

Freddie grew up in Salford, near the old Salford Hippodrome. The manager ('a fella called Percy Broadhead — a lovely man with a big bushy beard') used to book Freddie's granddad, so he used to let Freddie in for

Above and overleaf **Freddie 'Parrot Face' Davies as his TV alter-ego Samuel Tweet.**

free. 'If he saw me in the interval he'd give me a packet of crisps and an ice cream.' One week, Freddie ended up playing the stooge for a mad speciality act called Professor Sparks, who used to appear onstage with a huge machine which generated electricity. 'The best bit of the act was audience participation,' recalled the late great Charlie Chester. 'He would get a bunch of volunteers onstage to "bath" the Electric Baby. The more they dipped the flannel into the water to wash the metal baby the more the electricity would be amplified. Their contortions were very funny. Nowadays he'd be locked up.'[1]

'I stooged for him for an entire week, for twelve performances, and got ten shillings,' recalls Freddie. Freddie was disgusted. He thought he was going to get a fiver. But even this salutary lesson still didn't put him off. In 1957, when he was doing his National Service in the army up in Newcastle,

he went to see the Billy Cotton Band Show, featuring a young all-round entertainer called Des O'Connor. After the show Freddie went backstage and asked him how to get into showbusiness. 'I went to Butlins and became a Redcoat and then I did an audition at the Nuffield Centre,' said Des.

Freddie took his advice. He went to the Nuffield Centre, an ex-servicemen's club in London where Variety agents used to go to scout for new talent. He did a comedy magic act, cobbled together with a few jokes of his granddad's, but he didn't have any joy. Disappointed but not disheartened, he followed Des O'Connor's other tip, and auditioned for Butlins. Like Des, he became a Redcoat, serving his apprenticeship at Butlins in

Skegness, alongside a young unknown comic from Ireland called Dave Allen. The drummer in the house band was a Liverpudlian called Richard Starkey, aka Ringo Starr.

Freddie went into Butlins in 1958 as a bingo caller and came out in 1963 as a fully-fledged stand-up comic. By now Variety was on its last legs, so he started playing the working men's clubs. They were huge barns, these places, often converted cinemas, which staged wrestling as well as comedians, some-times in the same show. For the comics, there were no in-betweens. You either died on your arse or you ripped the roof off.

These clubs were brash and boozy, but they weren't all rough and tumble. The top club was Jimmy Corrigan's Batley Variety Club, where Eric had his first heart attack, onstage in 1968. Freddie played there in 1967, a week after it opened, alongside Val Doonican. Subsequent acts included stars like Shirley Bassey, the Bee Gees, Louis Armstrong and Roy Orbison. It was all done on a grand scale, with every headliner a household name, but these showbiz legends were still all introduced by the club chairman, rather than a proper compère, just as they would be in any working men's club.

Eric and Ernie never really relished playing these sorts of places, but the fact that they could play them, and play them really well, says a lot about their pedigree as a proper front-of-curtain turn. 'They were essen-tially a theatre act, a live act,' says Freddie. 'While they managed to trans-fer to television, in the main, they were really marvellous live.' Freddie saw a side of them onstage that the rest of us only ever glimpsed on telly. 'They had a great affinity,' he says. 'The best double acts always have eye contact with one another. They know where they're going with a routine. If you watch a really good double act work together, the straight man will always know how far to take a routine. The people that make the best straight men are usually comics, because they know where the laugh is.' Ernie had been a comic, before he teamed up with Eric, and Freddie could see that he wasn't just a feed. 'Ernie was a very funny man. He knew where the laughs were.'

CHAPTER 22

KEN DODD

IN THE SUMMER OF 1955, the boys returned to Blackpool, but this time they were top of the bill, at the Central Pier. Supporting them was a young comic who'd made his professional debut less than a year before, but was already making a big impact around the halls. He was Professor Yaffle Chuckabutty, Operatic Tenor and Sausage Knotter, otherwise known as Ken Dodd.

'When the boys came back to Swansea to do *Babes In The Wood* they were slightly chastened, because they'd received quite a cuff round the ear from Dodd,' recalls Alan Curtis, who appeared with Eric and Ernie in pantomime the following Christmas. 'They couldn't hold their own with Dodd. He was so on the ball, and this marvellous material! Everyone was talking about Ken Dodd. Eric told me in a moment of confidence and absolute truth, "We couldn't keep up with him! An absolute powerhouse of jokes and gags!"'

*　　*　　*

Ken Dodd made his professional debut at the Nottingham Empire in 1954, but like Eric and Ernie, his timeless humour stretches even further back. By then he was already twenty-seven, only a couple of years younger than Eric and Ernie. He'd been semi-pro since his teens. He grew up with great Variety entertainers like Arthur Askey, Frank Randle and Robb Wilton. He's our last living link with that lost world, whose death throes were captured by John Osborne, in his greatest play, *The Entertainer*. And that's why Doddy is far more than just another light entertainer. He's a sort of Light Ent time machine. 'Ken Dodd is the last music-hall comic that we have,' said Eric.[1] And he still is.

'When I first went to Blackpool in 1955, there were over twenty shows – twenty! – from Fleetwood to Lytham St Annes, employing probably about five thousand people,' Dodd tells me. 'We started at Easter and finished in November – twice nightly, three times on a Thursday.' Dodd closed the first half. Eric and Ernie closed the second. It was the perfect combination. 'They were a couple of wise guys and I was just a clown.' He's being modest. Dodd ripped the roof off the Central Pier that summer, and very nearly stole the show. Eric and Ernie were top of the bill, but they struggled to keep up with him. 'I don't think they'd found their identity,' he says. 'You go up all sorts of streets and all sorts of avenues until you find a place called home.'

However the atmosphere backstage was supportive rather than competitive. 'Everybody watched everybody else, partly for enjoyment and partly to see if you could learn anything.' And even though their acts were a world apart, they had a lot in common. 'We shared the belief that comedy was king, we loved the sound of laughter, and we had enthusiasm. We loved showbusiness. We loved the job. We couldn't wait to get on that stage and get cracking.'

It's Saturday night and I'm at the Plaza, an enormous old cinema in Stockport, shiny white in the winter drizzle. This vast art deco auditorium holds nearly 2000 people, yet tonight every seat is taken. However these punters haven't braved such filthy weather to watch the latest Edinburgh Festival sensation. They've come out on a cold wet evening to pay tribute to the last of the old-time entertainers. They've come to see Ken Dodd.

Taking your seat in the Plaza, you certainly feel like you're stepping back in time. There's even one of those beautiful old organs that rises up out of the floor. And yet the atmosphere isn't geriatric. It's frisky and full of fun. There's a sense of expectation in the air – excitement, even. You can sense they're waiting for someone special. And then Ken Dodd appears.

Doddy doesn't do shows. He does marathons. There's a singer and a magic act, and his juvenile chorus line, the Diddymen – but mainly, it's just him and a stand-up mike and about a billion gags. He's well into his seventies now, the sort of age most folk start slowing down, but tonight's show lasts over five hours, and you get the feeling he only finished then because we were tired – not him. 'I really don't think you're up to this,' he warns us, but when he calls it quits at a quarter to one, only a tiny fraction of this full house has scuttled off in search of late-night buses. The rest are on their feet – clapping, even cheering. And tonight is not unusual. He's always on the road, clocking up a hundred thousand miles a year. So what makes this buck-toothed clown so special, especially to audiences of a certain age?

One thing's for sure – it's not the material, it's the man. Ken Dodd has got some great gags in his enormous arsenal, but it's the bloke who's really funny, rather than the funny things he says. The sheer strength of his stage presence

Blackpool summer season: Eric and Ernie do the publicity bit with Ken Dodd. It wasn't just expected that artistes would go out on the front for photo opportunities, it was obligatory.

Ken Dodd outside the London Palladium, where the giant egg he is using to promote his 1965 Easter show has attracted the attention of a traffic warden.

wins you over, regardless of the gags, which are a mix of gems and groaners. He's a comic icon, in the same way that Morecambe & Wise were icons. With him, as it was with them, it's about more than just the laughs. He's the end of the line, the last of the Great British comics, and when he's gone, the comedy that Eric and Ernie knew will be gone for good.

Kenneth Arthur Dodd was born on 8 November 1927 in Knotty Ash, the Liverpool suburb that's become synonymous with his name. A lifetime later, he still lives in the seventeenth-century house where he was born, where his father worked as a coal merchant. Ken helped deliver coal, but it was the Punch & Judy show his parents bought him that inspired his career. He started doing shows in the back garden, and progressed to charity gigs at local fetes. By the time he left school at fourteen he'd already graduated to ventriloquism, working as a door-to-door salesman by day and playing concert parties after hours.

By the end of the Fifties he'd become a regular on the radio, but it was during the Sixties that he really made his mark. In 1965, he played an unprecedented forty-two week run at the London Palladium (twice nightly, three shows Saturdays) and had a Number One hit with 'Tears' — still one of the twenty best-selling records of all time.

'The funniest comedian you ever saw was my father,' says Dodd, speaking to me on the phone from his ancestral home in Knotty Ash. 'Sunday afternoon tea was a wonderful experience because when we'd had our pineapple chunks and cream, he'd start telling us jokes, pulling funny faces, telling us stories, putting on silly hats and singing silly little songs for us.' He also took

177

him to the theatre. 'That's where I fell in love with the lovely rosy, cosy glow of the stage,' he says. 'All small boys want to be an engine driver. The engine driver of every show, as I understood it, was this man who came on and told jokes and made the audience laugh.' He did his first show when he was a schoolboy, at an orphanage on Christmas Day. 'Once you've stood on a stage and you've won your first laugh and earned your first applause, you're hooked for life.' Nearly seventy years later it still hasn't left him. 'It's a wonderful way to spend your time, slaving over a hot audience.'

Once he was in the mainstream and the Edinburgh Festival was alternative, but now the tables have turned. 'The powers that be, the planners, have decided that Variety doesn't have a place on television or radio. We're more or less banned from it. We're not needed – at the moment.' He's confident the wheel will turn again one day, but it'll be a problem finding producers to stage these shows. 'The people who should be able to produce Variety aren't there. They don't know how to do it.' In the meantime, Dodd keeps packing them in, playing to the silent majority who adore him.

'You have to love an audience,' he concludes. 'You have to love people for all their silliness and for all the daft things we do, and find joy in being alive, not sneering and snarling and moaning and whinging about everything. Life is wonderful. Enjoy yourself. It's later than you think.'

Back in Stockport, back onstage, it's even later. 'God, I love this job,' he says, to himself as much as anyone. 'If you don't laugh at the jokes, I'll follow you home and shout them through your letterbox.' It's well past midnight, and the last bus has long since departed. 'All you need now is a lift home,' he says, but we're in no hurry to leave. 'I've been blessed in my life,' he says, intimate at last in front of a few thousand strangers. 'How many men get to work with their heroes?' He reels off a list of names – some famous, some long forgotten. He's almost talking to himself now, the rest of us listening in. As the curtain falls, the audience rise in a standing ovation.

Welcome Return

MORECAMBE

&

WISE

Presented by Kimbrell - Stepham Associates

Winter Gardens,
Bournemouth
Sunday,
9th August

Above **Eric and Ernie** do their bit at the opening of a supermarket.

Left **Eric and Ernie under orders to be less comic and more matinee idol.**

Above **There is absolutely no way you are going to get away with palming Ernie Wise a bouncing cheque.**

Below **Ernie takes bets on Eric being able to get his tiddlywink into the egg cup.**

CHAPTER 23

WYN CALVIN

WYN CALVIN WAS BORN in Pembrokeshire in 1928, two years after Eric and three years after Ernie. He came from a long line of Presbyterian preachers, and everyone assumed he'd go into the family business. 'Let him get it out of his system,' they said, when he went into the theatre. More than sixty years later, they're still waiting. Still, stand-up comedy isn't really all that different from preaching, and his MBE for charity work shows good deeds aren't confined to the pulpit. The Lord moves in mysterious ways, his wonders to perform, even on a wet Monday night, first house at the Glasgow Empire.

Like so many entertainers of his generation, Wyn got his first break in showbusiness thanks to a failed Austrian landscape painter called Adolf Hitler. In 1945, straight from school, Wyn joined ENSA, the Entertainments National Service Association (aka Every Night Something Awful) and set off for the

Continent, to entertain the troops. He had to wear uniform. Otherwise, if he'd been captured, he would have been shot as a spy, rather than imprisoned as a PoW. 'As a callow, teenage, pimply youth, the day that I was put into that pseudo-military uniform, Hitler committed suicide, so you can see the impact of putting me into khaki!' The Führer clearly realized the game was up.

Wyn was booked to play the juvenile lead, but when the principal comic was sent home for liberating a large quantity of German wines and spirits, Wyn was required to take his place. However he still hadn't given up on the idea of becoming a proper actor, and when he returned to Blighty at the end of this tour of duty, he went into weekly rep. Wyn clearly wasn't cut out for a career as a serious thespian. Even when he was playing the romantic lead he kept on getting laughs. Eventually he took the hint and went into Variety as a second-spot comic. Billed as The Welsh Prince of Laughter, he played countless summer seasons, including seven summers at Llandudno and five on

Blackpool's Central Pier. He also appeared in numerous pantomimes, starting off as Buttons and ending up as the Dame.

He first met Eric in Morecambe back in 1948. Eric had a week off (he actually had quite a few weeks off in those days) and had come home to see his mum and dad. Even when his career was at its lowest ebb, he still managed to make Wyn laugh. Wyn was in weekly rep, appearing in a play every evening and learning another during the day. 'You were performing this week's play, rehearsing next week's play, trying to get sight of the play for the week after, trying to forget the one you did last week.'

Wyn next met up with Eric (and Ernie) in Bournemouth in 1954. They were top of the bill by now, but Wyn found them in the doldrums, still smarting from the failure of their first series, *Running Wild*. The boys were doing well, but they weren't big names, and their act was solid rather than sensational. Wyn was the second-spot comic. There were six other acts on the bill. 'There were eight acts on those bills,' says Wyn. 'Every one different – that's why it was called Variety.' This gruelling slog was a great way of polishing a live act, but it didn't count for much on telly. 'Twice nightly, week after week, you honed a performance to perfection. Every television performance is a first night and a last night.' That's why most Variety acts never really felt at home on telly, and back then it still looked as if Morecambe & Wise would be one of them. So why did Eric and Ernie succeed (eventually) where so many

other fine acts failed? Well, firstly, they were always different, even when they weren't quite the finished article. 'They weren't like any of the established double acts of the time. They were younger and brighter, and they had a different slant on comedy. They were energetic and they moved well, but not in a knockabout style. They were a bit more sophisticated.'

Secondly, they got along with each other much better than most double acts. 'So many double acts of the time were always put into dressing-rooms together and treated as an entity rather than two different individuals. In the end they got on each other's nerves and would break up. That wasn't so with them. They interacted socially with each other. They didn't go the way of so many double acts, who couldn't stand each other. There wasn't that personal antipathy. That didn't develop with them.'

And thirdly, they simply worked far harder than most performers. They weren't great writers of comedy but they were great collectors, and they were always open to new ideas, long after other acts their age had settled into a familiar rut. One winter, Wyn was in pantomime in Cardiff, while the boys were in panto in Bristol. Since their matinées were on different days, Wyn went over to Bristol one afternoon to see their show. He went backstage for a chinwag, but he found that even in the dressing-room, they were always on the lookout for new material. 'That's a good gag!' Eric said, when Wyn told them a funny story. 'Ernie! Make a note of that!'

Wyn last met up with Eric at Luton Town Football Club, a few years before Eric died. Wyn was doing some after-dinner speaking. Eric was there in his capacity as Luton's most famous fan. By now Eric and Ernie were huge stars, thanks to their successful transfer to TV, a transfer that, for all his success in so many other fields, Wyn Calvin never mastered. 'A theatre performer does not necessarily make a television performer,' he says, without any rancour. 'They are two completely different techniques. They mastered television. Because of the amount of radio that I've done, I've been able to make a friend of a microphone. I've never been able to make a friend of a camera. They made a friend of a camera.' And the reason they made that influential friend had an awful lot to do with a man called John Ammonds.

Eric and Ernie engage in a bit of friendly horseplay, competing to get their face into the lipstick television screen.

CHAPTER 24

JOHN AMMONDS

NINETEEN FIFTY-THREE HAD BEEN A BUSY YEAR for Eric and Ernie. Ernie got married, Eric became a dad, and the boys did their first radio series, *You're Only Young Once*. It was made by the BBC in Manchester, one episode every Sunday — their only day off, since they were performing in Variety all around the country every other day of the week. They'd arrive on Sunday morning, rehearse the show during the day, and record it that evening at the Hulme Hippodrome, in front of a live audience. Despite this frantic schedule, the first series went down well and they were booked to do a second. The producer of this series was John Ammonds, the man who, many years later, produced and directed the TV shows that made them household names.

Above **John Ammonds, BBC Producer of** *The Morecambe & Wise Show,* **flanked by the boys.**

Ammonds cemented the partnership between Morecambe & Wise and their great scriptwriter Eddie Braben, but his most inspired move was to transport the warmth of Eric and Ernie's live Variety shows on to TV. Ammonds shot *The Morecambe & Wise Show* on a wooden stage, with velvet curtains, giving their TV recordings the atmosphere of an authentic theatre show. However he also understood the ways in which TV differs from the theatre. He used lots of close-ups, and encouraged Eric to confide in the camera. The resultant intimacy was fundamental to the show's huge appeal.

Ammonds rehearsed painstakingly with Morecambe & Wise in a spartan community centre in west London, polishing their sketches until they seemed spontaneous. He also persuaded some of the biggest names in showbusiness to appear alongside them, including Rudolf Nureyev, Laurence Olivier and, most memorably, André Previn (Previn: 'You're playing all the wrong notes.' Eric: 'I'm playing all the right notes, but not necessarily in the right order.') Ammonds also devised the dance with which Eric and Ernie closed the show, inspired by Groucho Marx. 'Groucho had performed this peculiar dance and I proceeded to do it round the rehearsal room. They both collapsed laughing and they did it in the next show, after "Bring Me Sunshine".'

John Ammonds was born in London in 1924. He joined the BBC straight from school as a sound-effects operator, after answering an advert in the paper, and arrived at the BBC's Light Entertainment Department in 1941. During the Blitz, the Light Ent Department was evacuated to Bristol, and then to Bangor, where he worked with one of Eric and Ernie's favourite comics, Robb Wilton, and did sound effects for *ITMA* (It's That Man Again) with Tommy Handley, broadcast live every week to an audience of fifteen million.

John joined the army in 1943, worked for Army Broadcasting in Hamburg, and returned to London and the BBC as a studio manager in 1947. He worked with comedians like Terry-Thomas and Ted Ray, and in 1953 he went back to the Light Ent Dept, this time in Manchester. It was here that he met up with Eric and Ernie. 'They used to come up on the Sunday morning at about ten,' he says, still lively in his early eighties. 'We'd meet at the old Broadcasting House in Piccadilly.' We're sitting in his smart flat out in the Home Counties commuter belt. There are birds singing in the trees outside.

'It was a bit of a one-man band,' says John, as we listen to an ancient recording of *You're Only Young Once* – or 'YoYo', as it became known. 'It was all done on the day – we rehearsed and then recorded it.' After more than fifty years, Eric and Ernie still sound incredibly fresh and chirpy – even more fresh and chirpy, in fact, than they were in their TV prime. 'They worked terribly hard,' says John. 'It really was a remarkable piece of work. And of course, I got to know them pretty well.' Their broadcasting experience still only amounted to a few bits and pieces (only radio – no telly, not yet) but John was staggered by their immense experience of live Variety. They'd been professional comedians for fifteen years, and they were still both the right side of thirty.

YoYo was a big success, but only up north. It was never even broadcast down south. The boys were doing well by now, but although they were well known around the halls they were still far from famous. They were never a broad northern act (not like Eric's Lancastrian idol, Robb Wilton, or Ernie's fellow Yorkshireman, Harry Worth) but until TV took them up, they were bigger in the north than they were down south. Northern audiences have always liked their comics amiable and bumbling, like George Formby. Southern audiences have always liked their comics sharp and cutting, like Max Miller. Miller was a high-status act (you'll like me, I'm something special). Formby was low status (you'll like me, I'm just like you). Unlike a lot of northern comics, Eric and Ernie's accents weren't too strong for southern audiences to understand, but their affectionate sense of fun was still far more northern than southern. Radio was starting to blur this north–south divide (audiences were becoming more accustomed to hearing regional

CHATHAM EMPIRE

PRESENTS

MORECAMBE & WISE

WITH THEIR ALL LAUGHTER SHOW!

"YOU'RE ONLY YOUNG ONCE"

•

PROGRAMME - - THREEPENCE

The Chatham Empire was one of the theatres on the variety hall circuit you had to be seen on to get your career up and running.

accents, for one thing) but at that time they were still better known north of Stockport.

From 1958, Ammonds worked as a TV producer, masterminding Harry Worth's debut in situation comedy, and in 1964 he produced Val Doonican's first TV series in Manchester. He returned to London when Doonican decided to bring the programme down south. The show attracted sixteen million viewers, and when Eric and Ernie moved from ATV to the BBC, Bill Cotton Junior, Head of Variety, asked Ammonds to produce and direct their show. When Ammonds started with *The Morecambe & Wise Show* in 1968, Eric and Ernie were familiar national figures. By the time he left the show, six years later, they had become national treasures. In the New Years Honours in 1975, Ammonds was awarded the MBE.

Ammonds subsequently produced comics such as Les Dawson, Jim Davidson, Frankie Howerd and Norman Wisdom, plus entertainers like Max Bygraves and Marti Caine. In 1980 he rejoined Eric and Ernie, who were now at Thames TV. Despite his best efforts the shows that Eric and Ernie made for Thames never matched the brilliant shows they made for the BBC, and in 1983 he retired, to look after his wife, Wyn, who suffered from multiple sclerosis. These days she has to live in a nursing home (her devoted husband isn't getting any younger) but he visits her regularly, and though he lives alone in their marital home, it still feels like somewhere they share. They have a daughter and two grandchildren. There are photographs of Eric and Ernie all around his dapper apartment, but the family photos have pride of place.

'They were a joy to work with,' says John, as we say goodbye. 'They looked like they were making it up as they went along because they worked so hard.' Their humour only seemed so spontaneous because it was so painstakingly prepared. On the way out, he shows me a trophy – The Society of Film and Television Arts Special Award, 1970. Three names are inscribed on the base: Eric Morecambe, Ernie Wise and Eddie Braben. John went to the ceremony with Eric and Ernie, and waited at their table while they went up to collect it. When the boys returned to their table with the award, Eric handed it to John. 'Here,' he said. 'You keep it. It's about time you had one of these.'

Advertising knitwear.
This was a popular sideline
in the fifties and sixties.
Don't give up the day
jobs, boys.

Above **Eric and Ernie with their script writers, Sid Green (directly behind Eric) and Dick Hills (directly behind Ernie). This dates from their ATV Show days for Lew Grade, working on** *Two of a Kind*.

Below **Ernie enjoys himself looking through Eric's old family albums.**

CHAPTER 25

PEARL CARR AND
TEDDY JOHNSON

WHEN I GET BACK FROM JOHN AMMONDS' PLACE, I listen to the old recording he gave me. It's an episode of *You're Only Young Once*, recorded at the Hulme Hippodrome all those years ago. For fans of Morecambe & Wise, it's quite a find. Nobody down south even heard it in the first place. The original tapes have long since been wiped. 'This is the North of England Home Service,' declares a distinctly southern-sounding announcer, and then a less posh and plummy voice breaks in, and then another. They're so familiar you recognize them instantly, as if they were members of your own family.

'Is it true you can see the future in that crystal ball?' asks Ernie.

'Yes, watch!' says Eric. 'This is terrible! In seven days time your wife will run off with another man!'

'Will I be glad to see the last of her!' says Ernie. 'For years she's nagged me. No drinking, no smoking, no nights out. This is wonderful news!'

'You're not serious, are you?' asks Eric.

'I certainly am,' says Ernie. 'Tell me, who is the old battleaxe going to run away with?'

'Me!' says Eric.

It's all cracking stuff – as sharp as their TV shows, and still just as funny, over half a century later. Of course their comic characters aren't quite so rounded and well defined as they became in later years, and the routines are far more crude and rudimentary than the sophisticated TV sketches that Eddie Braben wrote for them. Yet all the wit and warmth that made them so adored in their heyday is already there. They're unmistakably Morecambe & Wise.

Harry Secombe's on the show as well, and he gets more applause than they do. Thanks to *The Goon Show*, he was already a big star, unlike Eric and Ernie.

Eric and Ernie's sometime co-stars Pearl Carr and Teddy Johnson.

Teddy's first week as a solo artiste in Variety, sharing the top of the bill in 1951, way above Morecambe & Wise.

'Gather round me,' says the tubby star. 'We can't,' says Eric. 'There's not enough of us.' Then they introduce another special guest, and I get another nice surprise. It's Pearl Carr, one of the top pop singers of the 1950s. In 1955 she formed a duo with her new husband, the singer Teddy Johnson, and in 1959, they came within a whisker of winning the Eurovision Song Contest with a song called 'Sing Little Birdie'. I make a few enquiries, and it turns out they're still around. Doreen Wise gives me their number (they were especially firm friends with her and Ernie — they often holidayed in Malta and Florida together) and the next thing I know I'm in their living-room, in their pretty house in Barnes on the south side of the River Thames. They're both bright and sprightly, and full of fascinating memories of all the times they worked with Eric and Ernie, and so much else besides.

Teddy Johnson was born in 1920, five years before Ernie. Pearl Carr was born three years later, in 1923. Pearl's mother had been a singer and a dancer in the old music halls, and so she taught Pearl to sing and dance. Pearl made her professional debut when she was just twelve years old, with a troupe called Terry's Juveniles. They danced at the Astoria cinemas, which staged strange hybrid shows called cine-variety. As the name implied, this was a bizarre amalgam of live Variety and cinema. Improbable as it sounds, it was quite popular, for a while. From dancing it was a short step to singing, and by 1942 she was appearing at the London Palladium, in a show called *Best Bib And Tucker* with Tommy Trinder. She was still only a teenager. Just around the corner, at the Prince of Wales, Sid Field was starring in *Strike A New Note* with Eric and Ernie and Sheila Mathews in the chorus.

Unlike Pearl, Teddy didn't come from a showbusiness family. His mother and father were fine amateur singers, but he really got hooked on showbiz listening to dance bands on the radio. He particularly liked Bing Crosby. 'He was the first singer ever to make a friend of the microphone,' says Teddy (Eric made a friend of the television camera in much the same way). Teddy learnt to play the drums on a borrowed kit, and at the age of fourteen he formed his own dance band. He started singing and drumming in church halls, for five shillings a night, and soon graduated to playing cruise ships — sailing all the way to Canada, Japan and Australia, stopping off in exotic places like Hong Kong and Singapore along the way. He'd never even been abroad before. Like Pearl, he was still in his teens.

Pearl Carr and Teddy Johnson doing their song and dance act in the 1968 theatre presentation of the *Morecambe & Wise Show*. This was a Variety show, sponsored by Ovaltine, and produced by the show business impresario Derek Boulton, who took this photo.

After the war, they both worked with some of Britain's best dance bands, but it was a few years before they met. By 1950, Pearl was one of the top singers in the country. Teddy, meanwhile, had been working as an announcer on Radio Luxembourg. People didn't call them disc jockeys then, but in a way he was Britain's first DJ. In 1950 he came back to Blighty, made some hit records, and became a singing star. Teddy shows me some old playbills. 'That was my first ever week in Variety,' he says, with quiet pride, handing me a stiff sheet of cardboard. It's for the week beginning 16 July 1951. The block capitals are still bold and bright, even after all these years. It's the line-up for the Finsbury Park Empire, one of London's finest Variety Theatres, built by the great Frank Matcham in 1910 and demolished in 1965. A block of flats stands on the site today. Top of the bill is Anton Karas, the zither player from *The Third Man*. Teddy is second-top. Then comes singing brothers Bob and Alf Pearson ('We bring you melody from out of the sky, my brother and I'). At the bottom of the bill (the so-called wines and spirits) are Morecambe &

Wise. 'They were virtually first-spot comics,' says Teddy. 'They had a spot early in the first half, which is where they used to blood new comics — unknown kids.' These were the gigs that made them great, the gigs where they gradually honed their act to perfection. 'You could die a death in Variety,' says Teddy. 'In Variety, you were able to experiment until you got something that was perfect.' Teddy passes me another playbill, from the Chiswick Empire, just up the road — another Frank Matcham masterpiece, torn down without a second thought. And there he is, in big block capitals, 'the outstanding Columbia Recording singing star, Teddy Johnson', alongside Benny Hill and Peter Sellers.

Offers flooded in, including a week's work as a stand-in straight man for the great American Jack Benny, and (far more important) an invitation to appear on a radio show called *Black Magic*, alongside the great (and very glamorous) Pearl Carr. The producer asked them to sing some duets together. 'I'm sorry,' said Teddy. 'I'm not a good enough singer to sing with Pearl Carr.' Thankfully, they talked him into it, and of course he didn't mind a bit. 'I admired her tremendously,' he says. 'I thought she was great.'

'I wouldn't say it was love at first, but we had eye contact,' says Pearl, with a twinkle. They were both seeing other people, so nothing came of it, but they became friends, and in 1954, she called him up. He was playing the notorious Glasgow Empire, alongside the legendary Wilson, Keppel and Betty and a couple of jobbing comics called Morecambe & Wise. 'It's a shame,' Pearl told him. 'You're going to be away on tour. I'll miss you.' 'Why don't you come with me?' said Teddy. 'You could close the first half and I could close the show, and maybe we could do a couple of numbers together at the

Pearl and Teddy sport a specially made and highly fashionable new wardrobe.

202

end of my act?' 'I never thought she'd say yes,' he tells me. But she did. They worked together from then on. 'People loved it,' says Pearl. They were married in 1955. Over fifty years later, they're still going strong.

In 1956 they appeared alongside Eric and Ernie on Winifred Atwell's TV show. Atwell was a West Indian pianist who'd become a star after switching from classical to boogie-woogie (though she eventually switched back again) and her show resurrected Eric and Ernie's TV career, after their first series, *Running Wild*, had flopped in 1954. Pearl and Teddy played a big part in making *The Winifred Atwell Show* a success, and from then on Eric and Ernie were regular guests on all sorts of Variety TV shows. However, right up until the late 1960s, live Variety remained their mainstay, and the greatest Variety theatre in the land was the London Palladium.

Eric 'wigged up' during Morecambe & Wise's appearance on *The Ed Sullivan Show*.

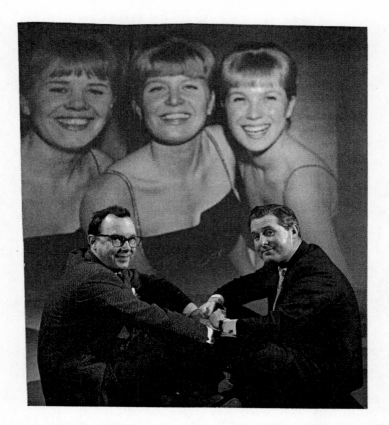

CHAPTER 26

BRUCE FORSYTH

'THE LONDON PALLADIUM was the most beautiful theatre to play in,' says Pearl Carr. 'It's one of those theatres that when you get on that stage and you look out at that audience, you really feel you've arrived.' Her husband, Teddy, agrees. 'Every time I've walked out on that stage at the Palladium, I've thought, "I'm in showbusiness for real!"' It was 1964, and Pearl and Teddy were playing the Palladium alongside Morecambe & Wise.

Eric and Ernie were in their late thirties now, and after more than twenty years in the business, they were an established act at last. Yet although they were on to their second series at ATV, eclipsing the failure of their first BBC series, *Running Wild*, they still weren't top of the bill. That honour went to an all-round entertainer called Bruce Forsyth. For the last thirty years he's been a TV institution, but like Eric and Ernie, he learnt his trade in live Variety, and this Palladium show was the end of a long climb up this greasy pole.

'There was always a dancing act to open the bill, and for five years I was the second-spot comic that went on after the dancing,' says Bruce, still just as lively in his late seventies as he was when he made his Variety debut, as Boy Bruce, The Mighty Atom, in his early teens. 'It can be the most frustrating spot on a Variety bill, because it's your job to warm the audience up.' For a performer who'd always oozed star quality, it was a painful apprenticeship. Bruce would warm them up a treat, but it was the other turns who reaped the benefit. He saw some wonderful acts from the wings, great comics like Max Miller and Jimmy James ('you could watch Jimmy's act every night and still laugh at it') but playing second-spot was pretty dispiriting all the same. 'I got so depressed doing it,' he says. 'You were more or less thrown to the lions. In some theatres it was a very difficult task, places like the Birmingham Hippodrome and the Glasgow Empire. They were very hard places to work if you were unknown and you were the first one who had to face this audience on a Monday, Tuesday, Wednesday night — especially the first houses, because there wasn't so many people there. I gave myself five years to make it and I got the job at the Palladium with only about six months to spare.'

There'd been some tough times along the way. During the war Bruce was playing the piano for a singer at the Shepherd's Bush Empire, where, years later, he filmed *The Generation Game*. 'This buzz-bomb came over and all of a sudden the engine stopped, which meant within five or six seconds the bomb would crash.' The audience all jumped under their seats. Bruce and the singer both got under the grand piano. The blast shook the theatre. Then they both got up and dusted themselves down and carried on with the show.

Being out of work was worse. 'A lot of the time I'd be broke,' he says, but unlike a lot of entertainers, he never starved. 'I had a wonderful mother and father who always looked after me,' he says. 'They kept me in the business. If I hadn't had their support I don't know whether I would have lasted in the business.' His mum always had great ambition for him, and his dad, who ran a garage, always gave him a drop of petrol for his car.

Bruce spent a year at the Windmill Theatre, where he fared better than Morecambe & Wise. Eric and Ernie had flopped in front of the dirty mac brigade, but doing six shows a day for a bunch of blokes who'd far rather be looking at naked ladies sharpened up Bruce's act no end. 'If somebody told you to do your act on the corner of Piccadilly Circus you'd just go on and do it, because you were tuned in to walking on and performing anywhere at any time.' From 1955 to 1957, he played three summer seasons at Babbacombe Concert Hall, a pretty little theatre on the clifftop above Torbay. Babbacombe is only a small resort, and to make sure holidaymakers kept coming back, the programme changed every three days. This hard work really honed his act, and it was here that he was spotted by Eric and Ernie's agent, Billy Marsh. In 1958, he became the principal compére of *Sunday Night At The London Palladium*, the TV show which brought Variety into people's living-rooms. He was thirty years old. He'd been in showbusiness for sixteen years.

'The Palladium was out of reach for most of us because it was the best in the world,' he says. 'If you were out of work, and most of us were in those days, you'd go along to the Wednesday matinée at the Palladium.' On Wednesday afternoons, Variety artistes could blag a free seat, so long as they showed their business card at the box office. In the post-war years, many of the headline acts were Americans, and one of Bruce's favourites was an American comic called Danny Thomas. Standing on the Palladium stage at the end of one midweek matinée, Thomas said something that stayed with Bruce throughout his long career. 'I know there's a lot of pros in this afternoon,' said Thomas. 'We're thrilled to have you here and it's always nice to be able to work in front of fellow professionals, but I would like to say one thing to you, especially if a lot of you are up-and-coming Variety artists. You can only be as good as your audience. You can never be better than them. You can be as good as they are, and if they're a bad audience, you can only be as good as a bad audience will let you.' Bruce never forgot these wise words, and as he approaches his eightieth birthday, he's still a master at getting the audience on his side.

Bruce Forsyth was born in 1928 and grew up in Edmonton, in north London. Every Wednesday, his mum and dad took him to the Wood Green Empire, and every Saturday to the Finsbury Park Empire. He could hardly have had a better introduction to live Variety. Wood Green was a Stoll theatre and Finsbury Park was a Moss theatre. Between them these two chains ran the best 'number one' theatres in the land. Below them was the 'number two' circuit, dominated by the Butterworth chain of theatres, and below that were the dreaded 'number threes'. 'I probably worked every third-rate theatre in this country,' remembers Bruce. 'Really dreadful, dreadful theatres with no atmosphere and awful bands. The band in some of these bad theatres was really awful, so when you did get up to the number ones and you worked in places like the Wood Green and Finsbury Park Empires, one of the thrills was hearing your music played correctly for the first time by a good orchestra, instead of a duff trumpet player and a rotten drummer and a conductor who didn't know where you were.' In those days he wasn't even thinking about TV. His one ambition was to play the number ones. On that circuit you were riding with the big boys. Anything could happen from there.

Sunday Night At The London Palladium made Bruce a star, and when he returned to the theatres where he'd played second-spot, he discovered it was a different story being top of the bill. The management were more attentive. Even the dressing-rooms were smarter. 'You never had to climb six flights of stairs,' he says. 'The manager would come round and see if you needed anything. It was not just a step up. It was a step above everybody else.' But the biggest difference was onstage. Gone were the days of warming up the house for other acts. 'All the other acts would go on and warm it up for you.'

When he played the Palladium with Eric and Ernie, Bruce was the headline act, but he always knew the boys were special, and he paid them the greatest compliment that one entertainer can pay another. Rather than retiring to his dressing-room, he used to watch them from the wings, just like he had done with Max Miller and Jimmy James. 'They had the same quality as Laurel and Hardy,' he says. 'Whatever they went through, you felt for them. You wanted them to be good. You wanted them to finish on top. You wanted everything to go right for them because you loved them, and that's what it's all about.' He'd always enjoyed their act, but now he could sense it had moved up a level, and he could tell that the audience could sense it too. 'I was thrilled to witness their sudden big leap into stardom,' he says.

After that London Palladium show, Eric and Ernie never looked back, and it was no coincidence that it was in this unique theatre, alongside this unique entertainer, that they bridged that great divide between stage and stalls and conjured up that strange illusion which is the common currency of stardom. Audiences had always liked them, but now they felt as if they knew them. 'That was the making of them,' says Bruce. 'I was thrilled for them because I'd worked with them quite a bit in the old days, and to see them finally get the recognition that they really deserved, it was very gratifying for me.' Fittingly, Bruce subsequently appeared in one of Eric and Ernie's celebrated Christmas shows, playing Father Christmas to Eric and Ernie's reindeer.

Morecambe & Wise's first venture into cinema: *The Intelligence Men*.

CHAPTER 27

MICHAEL GRADE

WHEN MORECAMBE & WISE finally hit the big time, Variety was already dying. At last they were top of the bill, but now the theatres where they'd learned their craft were closing, one by one. A lot of these Palaces and Empires were still making decent money, but their owners had discovered they could make a much quicker profit by selling off the city-centre plots they stood on. And so, for most of these theatres, that was that.

Despite all the showbiz bonhomie and camaraderie (or maybe even, in some way, because of it) Light Entertainment has always been a particularly brutal business. Trying to entertain a bunch of strangers is a uniquely precarious way to make a living, and with so much sentiment onstage, there's not a lot left over for real life. The theatres where Eric and Ernie had honed their act were bulldozed to make way for supermarkets and multi-storey car parks. These buildings had been put up for no higher purpose than to make money. Now they were worth more dead than alive.

London fared a bit better than most cities. It lost a lot of theatres, but it had many more to lose. The Chiswick Empire closed in 1959 and the Finsbury Park Empire in 1960. For a few years it lingered on as a rehearsal-room and scenery storeroom, until the bulldozers put it out of its misery in 1965. Outside the capital, the prognosis was even more gloomy. The Sheffield Empire shut up shop in 1959, the Cardiff Empire was torn down in 1962, and in 1963 the Glasgow Empire bit the dust, mourned, like an irascible old uncle, by all the English entertainers it had tormented.

Some theatres escaped the wrecker's ball, and a handful eventually even prospered, thanks to the tireless efforts of enthusiastic amateurs and a few far-sighted local councillors. The Belfast Opera House is still there, despite

the battering it took during the Troubles. Blackpool's Grand Theatre, another Frank Matcham masterpiece, was finally restored to its former glory, and still stages old troopers like Ken Dodd.

In London, theatres had to adapt to survive. The Shepherd's Bush Empire became a TV studio. Today it's a thriving rock venue. The Coliseum, built as a vast Variety theatre in 1904, is now the home of English National Opera. The Palladium is still there, of course, though now it mainly stages musicals. The Hackney Empire became a bingo hall, before being rescued and revived as a bastion of the Alternative Comedy scene.

Variety could have been preserved and nurtured, like live theatre, but even its biggest fans could see that the quality had been slipping for quite a while. So what went wrong? After all, the end, when it came, was remarkably sudden. In the late 1940s, cinemas were being converted into Variety theatres, to feed the growing demand for live (rather than recorded) Light Entertainment. Yet by the late 1960s, Variety had virtually disappeared.

Before the war, Light Ent Luddites used to worry that radio would kill off live Variety. In fact it did the opposite, drawing listeners to the theatres to see acts they'd only heard before. Curiously, however, TV didn't have quite the same effect. 'Radio filled theatres,' says the Welsh comic Wyn Calvin. 'Television emptied them.' A TV star was guaranteed a good audience and a fat fee in Variety, but the acts who hadn't made the grade on telly suffered in the halls. The best TV entertainers weren't always best at entertaining a live audience, and without TV exposure the best live entertainers found it increasingly hard to draw a crowd. Theatres that couldn't afford TV stars became increasingly dependent on nudes, driving the families away.

With big money flooding in from the networks, TV stars started demanding bigger and bigger fees from the theatres. The big theatres paid up, knowing these stars would attract an audience, and balanced the books by

Ernie points out to Eric that he's wearing the wrong trousers.

cutting costs further down the bill. Inevitably, the shows suffered. However big the headline act, Variety had always been a team game.

Actors experienced many of the same problems as Variety entertainers in the 1960s, and weekly rep largely vanished, along with twice-nightly live Variety. However, here in class-bound Britain, drama has long been regarded as high art, while Variety has always been dismissed as mere vulgar entertainment. Serious theatre was called legitimate theatre for a reason. Variety theatre was illegitimate, straight theatre's bastard son. Proper plays were a national asset, worthy of royal patronage and state subsidy. Variety was just as big a part of our cultural heritage, arguably even bigger (how many British comics can you name, and how many British playwrights?) but because it was working class, it was simply left to sink or swim.

There was a growing sense that the game was up, and unlike most Variety acts, Eric and Ernie weren't too scared to admit it. 'Albert Saveen is on at the moment,' wrote Eric in his diary, backstage at the ABC Theatre in Great Yarmouth, where he was appearing in summer season in 1967. 'I knew Albert twenty years ago and he's still doing the same thing. It's very sad.' Saveen was a

classic speciality act, a ventriloquist who'd learnt to breathe through either lung in turn while recuperating in hospital after suffering respiratory damage during the war. He had a real dog that really spoke (nobody could quite work out how he did it) and a doll called Daisy May who had her own bank account and phone number. Sometimes, Daisy would answer the phone, and flatly refuse to put callers through to Albert. 'I'll ask Mr Saveen to phone you back,'[1] she'd say. Sure enough, Albert would phone back, as if nothing had happened. Terribly charming, but a bit quaint in the year of *The Graduate* and *Sergeant Pepper*.

It wasn't just the acts who were beginning to look their age. The theatres had seen better days, and so had the resorts. 'Yarmouth really is a most terrible place,' wrote Eric in his diary. 'If cleanliness is next to godliness, in Yarmouth it's next to impossible. Outside the ABC stage door is a market, and at the end of the day there is so much paper and old fish and chips, as there are about six fish, chip and pea stalls belching out terrible smells eighteen hours a day. But the public put up with all this dirt.' They wouldn't for much longer. Unlike most of their colleagues, Eric and Ernie could see the future lay in television, and the men who did most to shape their TV destiny were Louis and Lazarus Winogradsky, better known as Lew and Leslie Grade. 'Knock knock, who's there?' went the old showbiz joke. 'Lew and Leslie!' 'Lew and Leslie who?' 'No wonder you don't get any work!'

Louis Winogradsky was born in the Ukraine in 1906. In 1912 his family fled to London to escape the Jewish pogroms. His father became a cinema manager and the family settled in what was then the Jewish ghetto of London's East End. In 1926, Lew won a Charleston contest at the Royal Albert Hall, and became a professional dancer. Realizing British audiences would find Winogradsky a bit of a mouthful, he shortened his surname to Grad. It was due to a printing error that he ended up as Lew Grade.

Lew's younger brother Boris soon followed him onstage. To avoid confusing audiences (though not subsequent biographers) Boris decided to call himself Bernard Delfont. In 1933, Lew started working as an agent, and in 1939 his youngest brother Leslie followed suit. Bernard started putting on musicals, and in 1942 he teamed up with an agent called Billy Marsh. Bernard became Britain's greatest theatrical impresario, while Lew became Britain's biggest TV mogul. And so when Eric and Ernie realized that live Variety was dying, they wrote to Billy Marsh and asked if he would take them on. Billy said he would. It was a wise decision, on both sides. Marsh's London Management was one of the best agencies in the business, and one of his brightest young colleagues was Leslie's son, a former sports reporter called Michael Grade.

Michael Grade first saw Eric and Ernie at the London Palladium, supporting Bruce Forsyth. 'They were brilliant stage performers,' he recalled, when I met him at the BBC, just a few days before he announced his resignation as chairman of the corporation, to return to ITV. 'The previous famous double act that came through the music halls was Jimmy Jewel and Ben Warriss, about whom Eric and Ernie were always very generous, although they were chastened by the fact that Jimmy and Ben, in the end, fell out. They were determined that they would never fall out.'

Of course, in any double act of such long standing, the odd row was unavoidable. As Grade says, it was like a marriage. But whatever rows Eric and Ernie had, nobody was ever allowed to see them quarrel. 'I think they were haunted by the spectre of the double acts that had fallen out with each other, and ended up bitter, not talking to each other.'

Eric and Ernie had always been big fans of Jewel and Warriss, but Grade could see their acts were worlds apart. 'Jimmy and Ben were huge stage performers, and they used to work in a very old-fashioned way,' says Grade. 'They very rarely talked to each other. They would have a conversation, but they'd be facing out towards the audience. It was a kind of old-fashioned vaudeville style, whereas Eric and Ernie were very intimate. They turned in and they looked at each other. They looked each other in the eye.' This naturalistic style allowed them to transfer their act to TV, whereas more stagey duos like Jewel and Warriss always looked awkward on the one-eyed god.

Eric and Ernie were quite content to be regarded as an old-fashioned Variety act, but although their humour harked back to music hall, their nose-to-nose delivery was innovative, especially on a big stage like the Palladium, where the house style has always been Teeth And Tits To The Gods. 'Although they were creatures of the vaudeville theatre, it was quite a modern style,' says Grade. 'It was quite radical.' Unlike a lot of double acts they realized their relationship was far more important than the gags. Their act was a two-man sitcom, rather than two stand-up comics cracking jokes.

Grade's father, Leslie, used to book Eric and Ernie in summer season, and when Michael began working for Billy Marsh, he went out on the road with them, to manage their spectacular seaside shows. 'The sense of anticipation in the theatre before the show started was unreal,' he says. 'The audience just couldn't believe how lucky they were.' From Yarmouth to Bournemouth, audiences all around the country responded to the affection that flowed between them. 'That relationship was very warm between the two of them, onstage and offstage, and that transmitted itself to the audience,' he says. 'They were very lovable. It's very important for a comedian to be lovable.' People could tell that Eric and Ernie had been through the same hard times as them, and that common ground gave them a special empathy with their punters. They'd survived the Blitz and the Depression. They'd endured rationing and conscription. They'd lived the same life as their fans, and now that fame had brought them a different lifestyle, their fans were pleased for them, rather than feeling alienated by their success. They weren't celebrities. They were kindred spirits.

Grade grew up with the gruelling routine of live Variety (fourteen shows a week – twice nightly, plus Saturday and Wednesday matinees) and he saw how that long apprenticeship gave Eric and Ernie a unique kinship with other entertainers, and each other. 'They knew how hard it was,' he says. 'They knew what a tough game it is to go out there every night, trying to earn a living making people laugh. What happens if they don't laugh? You haven't got a living.' Now Eric and Ernie were making big money, but that insecurity never left them. However big you were, there was always the same old worry: will they still laugh tonight?

The reason they laughed, and kept laughing, had an awful lot to do with Eric, but it had far more to do with Ernie than most people suppose. Watching them night after night, Grade could see that Eric was only ever as good as Ernie, and the reason Eric was always so good was because Ernie was always rock-solid. He was never just a feed ('in his own way, Ernie could be very funny') and his reliability gave Eric the freedom to be creative. Comedy is like music. It relies on form and rhythm. Eric made some wonderful melodies, but he'd have been lost without Ernie's bass lines.

Grade saw the act so often that in the end he could recite it word for word, and half a lifetime later, he can still recall all the highlights. One especially vivid memory is their mermaid routine. 'It was a silly sketch,' says Grade. 'Very broad, but very funny.' They'd dress up in stripy Edwardian bathing costumes (Eric would be wearing flippers) and Ernie would try (and fail) to teach Eric how to be a lifeguard. The sketch would finish off with Eric chasing a mermaid with a frying pan, shouting 'Frying tonight!' Yet the recollection that really lingers is them coming offstage in Yarmouth, bursting with excitement at having just broken in a brand-new bit of comic business. 'These mammoth stars were like children when they came off the stage,' he says. 'They'd found some new material. That was what meant so much to them.' They still hadn't lost that showbiz buzz, even after all those years.

'They never wasted anything,' says Grade. 'Everything they'd learnt, trooping round the music halls all those years, they'd find a use for somewhere. Everything they did, they learnt in the music hall. But where they were so smart was how they adapted those techniques to suit the television medium.' Variety was over. It was time to move on.

CHAPTER 28

ERNEST MAXIN

JOHN AMMONDS WAS THE PRODUCER who turned Morecambe & Wise into a top TV turn, but the man who choreographed their most memorable TV routines, with stars like Vanessa Redgrave, Glenda Jackson and Shirley Bassey, was Ernest Maxin. Like Ammonds, Maxin first encountered Eric and Ernie in the theatre, rather than on the floor of a television studio, and the TV shows he made with them harked back to the song-and-dance extravaganzas of their early days in live Variety, and the Hollywood musicals they'd watched

The Fab Six! The Beatles meet Eric and Ernie prior to appearing on *The Morecambe & Wise Show* in 1963.

Eric and Ernie dress up for the 1966 Royal Variety Show.

in the cinema when they were boys. 'I've always been MGM mad,' he says, sitting on the sofa in his plush apartment in Woodford, on the leafy edge of London, a home he shares with his elegant wife. 'I love the glamour and the gloss.' And as Eric and Ernie's choreographer (and eventually their producer), he brought the same gloss and glamour to Morecambe & Wise.

Ernest Maxin was weaned on showbusiness. His grandmother ran a theatrical boarding house in Leeds, and his mother spent her childhood helping out in the kitchen. His father played the violin. Ernest was born in Upton Park in east London (no wonder he's a West Ham fan) and began his stage career when he was just six years old, playing the piano, all blacked up, in a touring

'Me and my shadow', a song Eric and Ernie often performed on stage.

minstrel show. He played from Plymouth up to Glasgow, and all points in between. Most six-year-olds would have been terrified. Not him. 'I loved it,' he says. You can tell he's still in love with showbusiness today.

Ernest didn't just play the piano. He also learnt to dance, and every morning he'd be in the theatre, watching the acrobats rehearsing, and learning new tap-dance routines. However, his Variety career hit the buffers when he was nine years old. He was waiting by the stage door of the Sheffield Empire, killing time between shows, when he overheard the show's producer talking to his parents on the phone. 'I'm sorry,' Maxin heard him say. 'I'm afraid Ernest is washed up in the business. He's not getting the laughs any more.'

Maxin went back to school, but the showbiz bug never left him. He carried on playing the piano in the evenings and when he left school he became an actor. He also earned a bit of money as a professional boxer, fighting in famous East End venues like York Hall. When he was nineteen he went out to Australia to play the juvenile lead in a Variety show alongside Arthur Askey. They were touring with a production of *A Streetcar Named Desire*, starring Vivien Leigh (who won an Oscar for her performance in the film) and when the male lead had to return home, Maxin took over the role. Some BBC executives travelled out to Australia to try and persuade Leigh to do some work for them. Leigh wasn't interested, but Maxin was, and so he joined the BBC.

Maxin worked with American comedians like Jack Benny, and then the great theatrical impresario, Bernard Delfont, asked him to produce a couple of his summer shows, on the North Pier in Blackpool, with Tommy Cooper, and at the Princess Theatre in Torquay, with Morecambe & Wise. Maxin had seen Eric and Ernie performing in Variety theatres like the Chiswick Empire, long before they reached the top of the bill, so he was already a fan. Now, working with them, he could see what those years of toil had taught them. 'They knew how the other one breathed,' he says. 'Their timing was perfect.' He also saw the ways in which they supported and complemented each other. 'Eric was more of a worrier. Ernie was the calming influence.' And it was this blend of sangfroid and perfectionism which made them such a winning team. By now, they were getting standing ovations every night.

Three snaps taken on Eric's camera during location filming for *That Riviera Touch*.

CHAPTER 29

DAVID AND
PAULINE CONWAY

AFTER ERIC'S FIRST HEART ATTACK, in 1968, Eric and Ernie cut right back on their live work and focused on TV, but they were far too steeped in Variety to give it up completely. Instead of long runs in pantomime or summer season, they confined their live appearances to a series of lucrative one-night stands which they nicknamed bank raids. There were other entertainers on these bills, just like an old twice-nightly show in Variety, and remarkably, more than twenty years after Eric's death, and nearly ten years since Ernie's, some of those acts are still hard at it. I wanted to finish this book by writing about an act that's still working, rather than one that's retired or resting, so I was delighted to track down a musical duo called David and Pauline Conway. They supported Eric and Ernie in their heyday, and they're still going strong today.

David is a sprightly and ageless man – boyish, almost elfin, a bit like Melvyn Hayes from *It Ain't Half Hot Mum*. His wife Pauline is similarly elegant, but tall and slim. You can tell they're both dancers. They live in an immaculate modern house near Bournemouth. The garage is full of railway memorabilia, which is fitting, because it was model railways which got David into showbusiness.

When David was a kid in Coventry, one of the highlights of his week was the model railway club which met after school every Friday afternoon. Through this club he got his first job, in the local model shop, but this shop didn't just sell model railways. It sold harmonicas as well. The manager used to play the harmonica every morning in his office. David bought one for himself. It cost him thirty shillings – a week's wages – but it was money well spent. Within five years, he was playing professionally, on radio and TV, and in the Moss Empire chain of theatres – the top of the Variety tree. In 1961, after five years as a solo turn, he joined Britain's finest harmonica ensemble, The Monarchs. They'd seen him on TV, doing summer season in Whitley Bay. His first job with them was supporting Eric and Ernie's favourite double act, Jimmy Jewel and Ben Warriss. He was on his way.

Like Eric and Ernie, Pauline was a dancer from an early age. 'That's all I lived for,' she says, over coffee in her pristine kitchen. 'I was a contortionist as well.'

While she was still at school, in Wimbledon, she went for two auditions, both on the same day. One was for summer season in Felixstowe. The other was for *The Benny Hill Show* on TV. She got them both, but the authorities wouldn't let her do the television work because she was still only fourteen. However, they couldn't hold her back for long. She left school when she was fifteen, and she's been in showbusiness ever since.

Pauline and David met in 1967. They formed a double act (they never would have seen each other otherwise, since they were always working) and they've been together, professionally and personally, ever since. They worked with Dick Emery and Bob Monkhouse, and appeared in *The Black and White Minstrel Show* – much maligned nowadays, but like the minstrel shows of Eric and Ernie's youth, an important part of showbiz history. 'It was a great show,' says David, and there was no shortage of paying punters who felt the same way. 'We never, ever went into work thinking, "Will there be an audience?"' says Pauline. 'It was sold out every night, twice nightly.'

They first worked with Morecambe & Wise in 1976. The boys were huge by then, attracting TV audiences of over twenty million, and David and Pauline were very nervous. However, Eric and Ernie were the most unassuming stars they'd ever met. Before every show, they used to knock on all the dressing-room doors and say hello. This was a stark contrast to some other celebrities that David and Pauline had worked with. Some of the stars they'd worked for hardly said a word to them. However, Eric and Ernie had propped up a lot of bills, and they were better people (and performers) for it. Unlike a lot of so-called celebs, they never forgot where they were from. 'I think that's why they were loved so much,' says Pauline. 'There was a warmth there that I haven't seen in any other performers.' And their fans could see it too.

David and Pauline always got on well with Eric, but they became especially good friends with Ernie, and his constant companion, Doreen. 'Ernie and Doreen could see themselves in us,' says David, and I can see the similarity. Doreen and Pauline were both dancers. David and Ernie were both song-and-dance men. Neither couple had children. Maybe Ernie and Doreen saw in David and Pauline the couple they might have been, if Ernie hadn't become a big star. 'We had the same sort of attitude,' says Pauline. 'When we come offstage we are normal again, whereas a lot of artists cannot do that. They've got to be the artist offstage as well.' Unlike Eric and Ernie.

As they got to know Ernie better, David and Pauline soon realized he was far more than just a straight man. 'He always used to have a pen and some paper in his pocket,' recalls Pauline. 'We'd be talking, and something funny would happen, and he'd write it all down.' Often these snippets found their way into Eric and Ernie's routine. And as Ernie became a friend, they saw how funny he could be offstage. 'It's not bad for playing a mouth organ,' joked Ernie, looking around their home when he first visited them here. 'Think what you could have done if you'd been a good act.'

*   *   *

That evening David drives me into Bournemouth, where he's appearing in an end-of-the pier show. 'End-of-the-pier' has become a kind of umbrella term for a certain sort of trad entertainer, many of whom have never played a proper pier show in their lives. Yet tonight's show really is at the end of the pier, in one of the handful of pier theatres that still cling to the British coastline. As David has warned me, the audience is fairly sparse. Less than half the seats are taken, but like a true pro he doesn't let that put him off. He's a lovely mover, with feet that barely seem to touch the stage, and his patter's not bad either. 'Well, what do you expect for these prices?' he asks, rattling off a nifty rhythm on a set of bones. 'Altogether or not at all,' he says, as a smatter of applause interrupts a surprisingly tuneful melody upon a saw.

However, the highlight of his act is his harmonica. 'I always get asked, "Have you played the harmonica all your life?" Not yet. "Do you play the harmonica better than Larry Adler?" I do now.' But the self-deprecating humour stops as soon as he starts playing. The audience can tell he's in earnest now, and they give him the respect that he deserves. When David plays the harmonica, it sounds like a proper musical instrument, not a music-hall novelty, and he departs to the loudest (and longest) applause of the evening.

Tonight's music-hall nostalgia show has been an uphill struggle, and the other acts haven't managed to warm up a draughty room. However, you learn a lot more about entertainers on difficult nights than you do on easy ones, and tonight David Conway showed he still had what he had when Eric and Ernie booked him for their bank raids. When he leaves the stage, this audience feels alive at last, and though I fear for the future of this sort of show, and this sort of theatre, I don't feel any fear for him. 'Not bad for playing a mouth organ,' I think, recalling Ernie's quip, as I make my way back along the pier, towards the station, and the last train back to London. As I climb the hill, the lights outside the theatre are still winking — a faint glimmer of what they used to be, but still just about alive.

Opposite **Not a publicity shot but a family snapshot of Eric and Ernie at the Elbow Beach Hotel, Bermuda, where they holidayed with Joan and Doreen after appearing on** *The Ed Sullivan Show* **in New York.**

Left **Ernie captured by Eric while relaxing at Elbow Beach.**

Below **ATV scriptwriter Dick Hills and Ernie, waiting for Eric to get the car keys out.**

Below *Left to right*: Doreen, Dick Hills, Ernie, Eric and Joan, in New York.

Left **Three lovely ladies, with Eric bearing an uncanny resemblance to his mother, Sadie. The 'lady' in the middle is the renowned comic actor, Billy Dainty, who shared a life-long friendship with Mr and Mrs Wise.**

CHAPTER 30

ALAN RANDALL

THIS BOOK BEGAN WITH A LETTER from a dead entertainer, so it seems fitting to end it with one. Alan Randall was with Eric on the night he died. Alan was one of the great all-round instrumentalists of the Variety era. He could play the trumpet, the trombone, the piano and the vibraphone. He even played the drums, but the instrument which really made his name was the ukulele, particularly his immaculate impression of George Formby, Eric's idol and role model when he won that talent contest in Hoylake, which got him that audition with Jack Hylton, who introduced him to Ernie Wise. Alan wrote a personal account of Eric's last evening and gave it to Patrick Newley, the editor of *The Call Boy*, the journal of the British Music Hall Society, and obituarist to countless old Variety stars. Alan Randall has since died himself, so when Patrick heard I was writing this book, he kindly passed Alan's unpublished account of Eric's death on to me. This, more or less, is what he had to say.

In May 1984, just after his fifty-eighth birthday, Eric accepted an invitation from his old friend and Variety colleague Stan Stennett to do a question-and-answer session on the stage of the Roses Theatre in Tewkesbury. Stennett asked Alan Randall to do the music and book the band. Alan didn't know Eric well. He'd only worked with Eric and Ernie a few times, long ago, on the radio on *Workers' Playtime*. However, as luck would have it, he'd been on TV with Eric just a few weeks before, in a show called *Castles In The Air*, hosted by another old Variety pal of Eric's, Roy Castle.

When Alan arrived at the Theatre that afternoon, Eric was already there. Although it was nearly June, the weather was unseasonably chilly, and Alan was wearing a big black leather overcoat. 'Don't say you've brought your xylophone and set of drums on the back of a motorbike!' joshed Eric, when he saw him. 'Where have you parked? I'll give you a hand to bring them in!' Yet unlike a lot of stars, there was nothing condescending about his humour. 'Where's your dressing-room?' he asked Alan. 'I bet you haven't got one. You'd better come in with me.'

Like good old pros, the pair of them, they'd got there nice and early, so they had time to sit and chat in Eric's dressing-room for a couple of hours. They talked about football and show-business and Eric's retirement plans. Well, semi-retirement, anyway. Eric didn't want to do another TV series – he was sick of all the pressure – but he still planned to do the odd one-night stand. Tonight's show was a trial run for the sort of retirement show he had in mind. 'He talked to me as if he'd been a good mate for years,' reflected Alan, 'and yet I hardly knew him.' Eric said he'd like a nice little place in Bournemouth. He wanted to end his days beside the seaside, just like he'd begun them. Mind you, Bournemouth is a lot warmer than Morecambe, especially in the winter. Maybe that's why the people aren't so funny down there.

A waitress popped her head around the door and asked them if they wanted any drinks. A few beers before the show, or perhaps a drop of brandy? 'No thanks,' said Eric. 'But I'd love a big pot of tea.'

Eric did a storming show. He had the audience in stitches. During the interval he asked for another pot of tea to be sent round to his dressing-room. When Alan went on to do his solo spot, Eric stood and watched him from the wings, cheering him on. 'Go on lad!' he shouted. 'Let 'em have it!' When Alan began his closing routine, Eric joined him on stage, which was a complete surprise. When Alan played Scott Joplin's *The Entertainer* on the grand piano, Eric came and sat beside him and pretended to play along. When Alan started marching up and down the stage, banging on a big bass drum, Eric picked up another drum and marched along behind him. When Alan finished off on the vibraphone, Eric joined in with that as well. 'Which note do I play?' he asked. Alan showed him how to play a C. 'Is that it then?' asked Eric, with a wiggle of his glasses, as Alan brought the curtain down.

Eric walked towards the wings, but after a few steps he keeled over and fell to the floor. Alan knew it was serious straight away. The band was still playing. Alan ran back onstage and stopped them. Joan was sitting in the stalls, with Mrs Randall and Mrs Stennett. She knew something was wrong. Then came the announcement she'd been dreading. 'Is there a doctor in the house?' Her husband's name wasn't mentioned. It didn't matter. 'It's Eric,' she said. She rushed backstage. The audience shuffled out in silence. There was a doctor in the house, but there was nothing he could do.

At three o'clock in the morning, Stan rang Alan to say that Eric had died. Alan didn't sleep. At six o'clock that morning, the phone rang again. It was a reporter from one of the national newspapers. 'I believe you shared a dressing room with Eric Morecambe last night, and that you were onstage when he collapsed,' asked the journalist. 'Can you confirm that Eric Morecambe had been drinking heavily before he went onstage?' Alan was furious. He gave him an earful of abuse and slammed the phone down. Later that day, Alan got a phone call from George Bartram, Eric and Ernie's press agent. One of the theatres in the area had been in touch. They wanted to know if Ernie Wise would be available for pantomime.

In 1987, Ernie returned to the West End stage, for the last time, half a century after his West End debut, in a musical of Charles Dickens' unfinished final novel, *The Mystery of Edwin Drood*. 'I'm not a singer, I'm not an actor, but I've got a clog dance,' he said at the audition. Fifty years after he said goodbye to his old dad, and joined Jack Hylton, he was dusting down his old juvenile act again. He got the part. 'I'm trying to do a double act here on my own and not even getting paid for it,' he told the audience. Everyone laughed. Ernie was fine, and so was the show, but sadly it only ran for a few months. He never played the West End again. 'Can you think of a vehicle for him? Can anybody think of a vehicle for half of a big name?' asks Phil Rose, an actor who appeared with Ernie in the show. 'That's a bloody hard act to cast – a very hard act to cast.'

We're sitting in the Savage Club, the celebrated private club for entertainers (Arthur Askey, Tony Hancock, Tommy Trinder and Robb Wilton were all members) opposite the Playhouse Theatre, between the West End and the Thames. Phil and Patrick are reminiscing about Ernie, a man they both got to know a bit after Eric died. 'He did cut a very sad figure,' says Patrick, recalling the long epilogue of Ernie's career, which lasted for fifteen years from Eric's death in 1984, from a heart attack, aged fifty-eight, until Ernie's death in 1999, after a triple heart bypass, aged seventy-three. 'Even when he

appeared on TV programmes it was just one half, and audiences knew that. It was impossible for him to put across any kind of personality.' Nevertheless, there was one thing Ernie never lost, and that was his music-hall memories. 'You'll never guess who I saw the other day,' Patrick would say whenever he bumped into him. 'He's not still going, is he?' Ernie would reply. 'We did a bill with him!' It was always we, and he always remembered where and when. 'He retained a love of Variety for ever,' says Patrick, fondly. 'Variety was completely in their bones.' Now that world has gone for ever, we shall not see their like again. 'It was dying on its arse in the Sixties,' says Patrick. 'By the Seventies it was finished.' Only Morecambe & Wise remained, to show us all what we were missing.

Phil is from Manchester, where Eric and Ernie first set eyes on one another. 'I was there when they pulled down the Ardwick Hippodrome,' he says. 'I was there when they pulled down the Stretford Hippodrome. The last show at Stretford Hippodrome was a pantomime. Me dad, who was a bricklayer, he found it a bit hard in the winter – it were raining and whatever – he got a job backstage. At one point he was in charge of the Tumbling Waters – you know, the waterfall. We went to see it and it was packed. You couldn't get a seat for love nor money.' Phil was raised in Ardwick, just around the corner from the Hippodrome. As a lad, he sat and watched them pull it down.

'We loved Eric and Ernie – old people, young people, kids, everyone,' says Patrick, recalling that night in Croydon in 1973 when the boys recorded their live act for posterity. 'You felt that you knew them, totally. I can only say it was the same kind of love that people had for Laurel and Hardy.' Eric and Ernie would have liked that. For two northern lads who learnt their trade in the same theatres as Stan Laurel, there could be no higher praise.

Ernie: Have you got the maracas?
Eric: No, it's the way I walk.

NOTES

CHAPTER 1: RONNIE BARKER

1   Eric was just joking, of course. Frankie Howerd, one of England's most stately homosexuals, was never remotely interested in under-age males.

2   Tommy Cooper, though a great pal of Eric's, was notoriously tightfisted. *Sunday Times*, 16 December 1979

3   *There's No Answer To That! An Autobiography* by Eric Morecambe, Ernie Wise and Michael Freedland (Arthur Baker, 1981)

4   *There's No Answer To That! An Autobiography* by Eric Morecambe, Ernie Wise and Michael Freedland (Arthur Baker, 1981)

5   *Funny Way To Be A Hero* by John Fisher (Frederick Muller, 1973)

CHAPTER 2: ERIC BARTHOLOMEW

1   *Eric and Ernie – The Autobiography of Morecambe & Wise* by Eric Morecambe, Ernie Wise and Dennis Holman (WH Allen, 1973)

2   *Eric and Ernie – The Autobiography of Morecambe & Wise* by Eric Morecambe, Ernie Wise and Dennis Holman (WH Allen, 1973)

3   *Eric and Ernie – The Autobiography of Morecambe & Wise* by Eric Morecambe, Ernie Wise and Dennis Holman (WH Allen, 1973)

4   *Eric and Ernie – The Autobiography of Morecambe & Wise* by Eric Morecambe, Ernie Wise and Dennis Holman (WH Allen, 1973)

CHAPTER 3: ERNEST WISEMAN

1   *There's No Answer To That! An Autobiography* by Eric Morecambe, Ernie Wise and Michael Freedland (Arthur Baker, 1981)

2   *Still On My Way To Hollywood* by Ernie Wise (Duckworth, 1990)

3   *Eric and Ernie – The Autobiography of Morecambe & Wise* by Eric Morecambe, Ernie Wise and Dennis Holman (WH Allen, 1973)

4   *Still On My Way To Hollywood* by Ernie Wise (Duckworth, 1990)

5   *Still On My Way To Hollywood* by Ernie Wise (Duckworth, 1990)

6   *Eric and Ernie – The Autobiography of Morecambe & Wise* by Eric Morecambe, Ernie Wise and Dennis Holman (WH Allen, 1973)

7   *Eric and Ernie – The Autobiography of Morecambe & Wise* by Eric Morecambe, Ernie Wise and Dennis Holman (WH Allen, 1973)

8   *Still On My Way To Hollywood* by Ernie Wise (Duckworth, 1990)

CHAPTER 4: YOUTH TAKES A BOW

1   *TV Times*, 27 May 1965

2   *Still On My Way To Hollywood* by Ernie Wise (Duckworth, 1990)

3   *Eric and Ernie – The Autobiography of Morecambe & Wise* by Eric Morecambe, Ernie Wise and Dennis Holman (WH Allen, 1973)

4   *Eric and Ernie – The Autobiography of Morecambe & Wise* by Eric Morecambe, Ernie Wise and Dennis Holman (WH Allen, 1973)

5   *Roy Hudd's Cavalcade of Variety Acts – A Who Was Who of Light Entertainment 1945-1960* by Roy Hudd with Philip Hindin (Robson Books, 1997). This was at the London Palladium. The budget of *Youth Takes A Bow* didn't stretch to such spectacular (or expensive) beasts.

6   *Still On My Way To Hollywood* by Ernie Wise
    (Duckworth, 1990)

CHAPTER 5: MORECAMBE & WISE

1   *Eric and Ernie – The Autobiography of Morecambe
    & Wise* by Eric Morecambe, Ernie Wise and Dennis
    Holman (WH Allen, 1973)

2   *Eric and Ernie – The Autobiography of Morecambe
    & Wise* by Eric Morecambe, Ernie Wise and Dennis
    Holman (WH Allen, 1973)

3   *Eric and Ernie – The Autobiography of Morecambe
    & Wise* by Eric Morecambe, Ernie Wise and Dennis
    Holman (WH Allen, 1973)

4   *Still On My Way To Hollywood* by Ernie Wise
    (Duckworth, 1990)

5   *Still On My Way To Hollywood* by Ernie Wise
    (Duckworth, 1990)

6   *Eric and Ernie – The Autobiography of Morecambe
    & Wise* by Eric Morecambe, Ernie Wise and Dennis
    Holman (WH Allen, 1973)

7   *Eric and Ernie – The Autobiography of Morecambe
    & Wise* by Eric Morecambe, Ernie Wise and Dennis
    Holman (WH Allen, 1973)

8   *Eric and Ernie – The Autobiography of Morecambe
    & Wise* by Eric Morecambe, Ernie Wise and Dennis
    Holman (WH Allen, 1973)

9   *Eric and Ernie – The Autobiography of Morecambe
    & Wise* by Eric Morecambe, Ernie Wise and Dennis
    Holman (WH Allen, 1973)

CHAPTER 6: THE GLASGOW EMPIRE

1   *The People's Jesters – Twentieth Century British
    Comedians* by Eric Midwinter (Third Age Press,
    2006)

2   *Still On My Way To Hollywood* by Ernie Wise
    (Duckworth, 1990)

3   *The People's Jesters – Twentieth Century British
    Comedians* by Eric Midwinter (Third Age Press,
    2006)

4   *Eric and Ernie – The Autobiography of Morecambe
    & Wise* by Eric Morecambe, Ernie Wise and Dennis
    Holman (WH Allen, 1973)

5   *Eric and Ernie – The Autobiography of Morecambe
    & Wise* by Eric Morecambe, Ernie Wise and Dennis
    Holman (WH Allen, 1973)

6   *The People's Jesters – Twentieth Century British
    Comedians* by Eric Midwinter (Third Age Press,
    2006)

CHAPTER 7: STRIKE A NEW NOTE

1   *The People's Jesters – Twentieth Century British
    Comedians* by Eric Midwinter (Third Age Press,
    2006)

2   *Still On My Way To Hollywood* by Ernie Wise
    (Duckworth, 1990)

3   *The People's Jesters – Twentieth Century British
    Comedians* by Eric Midwinter (Third Age Press,
    2006)

4   *Eric and Ernie – The Autobiography of Morecambe
    & Wise* by Eric Morecambe, Ernie Wise and Dennis
    Holman (WH Allen, 1973)

5   *Eric and Ernie – The Autobiography of Morecambe
    & Wise* by Eric Morecambe, Ernie Wise and Dennis
    Holman (WH Allen, 1973)

CHAPTER 8: SHEILA MATHEWS

1   *Still On My Way To Hollywood* by Ernie Wise
    (Duckworth, 1990)

CHAPTER 9: LORD JOHN SANGER'S CIRCUS AND VARIETY

1   *Still On My Way To Hollywood* by Ernie Wise
    (Duckworth, 1990)

2   *Eric and Ernie – The Autobiography of Morecambe
    & Wise* by Eric Morecambe, Ernie Wise and Dennis
    Holman (WH Allen, 1973)

3   *Still On My Way To Hollywood* by Ernie Wise
    (Duckworth, 1990)

4   *Still On My Way To Hollywood* by Ernie Wise
    (Duckworth, 1990)

5   *Eric and Ernie – The Autobiography of Morecambe
    & Wise* by Eric Morecambe, Ernie Wise and Dennis
    Holman (WH Allen, 1973)

6   *Eric and Ernie – The Autobiography of Morecambe
    & Wise* by Eric Morecambe, Ernie Wise and Dennis
    Holman (WH Allen, 1973)

7   *Eric and Ernie – The Autobiography of Morecambe
    & Wise* by Eric Morecambe, Ernie Wise and Dennis
    Holman (WH Allen, 1973)

CHAPTER 11: WILSON, KEPPEL AND BETTY

1   *Eric and Ernie – The Autobiography of Morecambe
    & Wise* by Eric Morecambe, Ernie Wise and Dennis
    Holman (WH Allen, 1973)

2   *Eric and Ernie – The Autobiography of Morecambe
    & Wise* by Eric Morecambe, Ernie Wise and Dennis
    Holman (WH Allen, 1973)

3 *Eric and Ernie – The Autobiography of Morecambe & Wise* by Eric Morecambe, Ernie Wise and Dennis Holman (WH Allen, 1973)

4 *Still On My Way To Hollywood* by Ernie Wise (Duckworth, 1990)

5 *Still On My Way To Hollywood* by Ernie Wise (Duckworth, 1990)

6 *Kindly Leave The Stage! The Story of Variety 1919-1960* by Roger Wilmut (Methuen, 1985)

7 *Eric and Ernie – The Autobiography of Morecambe & Wise* by Eric Morecambe, Ernie Wise and Dennis Holman (WH Allen, 1973)

CHAPTER 12: THE WINDMILL STEEPLECHASE

1 *The Reluctant Jester* by Michael Bentine (Bantam, 1992)

2 *The Straight Man – My Life In Comedy* by Nicholas Parsons (Weidenfeld and Nicolson, 1994)

3 *The Straight Man – My Life In Comedy* by Nicholas Parsons (Weidenfeld and Nicolson, 1994)

4 *The Straight Man – My Life In Comedy* by Nicholas Parsons (Weidenfeld and Nicolson, 1994)

5 *The Reluctant Jester* by Michael Bentine (Bantam, 1992)

6 *Eric and Ernie – The Autobiography of Morecambe & Wise* by Eric Morecambe, Ernie Wise and Dennis Holman (WH Allen, 1973)

7 *Still On My Way To Hollywood* by Ernie Wise (Duckworth, 1990)

CHAPTER 13: FIG LEAVES AND APPLE SAUCE

1 *Still On My Way To Hollywood* by Ernie Wise (Duckworth, 1990)

2 *Still On My Way To Hollywood* by Ernie Wise (Duckworth, 1990)

3 *Eric and Ernie – The Autobiography of Morecambe & Wise* by Eric Morecambe, Ernie Wise and Dennis Holman (WH Allen, 1973)

CHAPTER 14: VOGELBEIN'S BEARS

1 *Eric and Ernie – The Autobiography of Morecambe & Wise* by Eric Morecambe, Ernie Wise and Dennis Holman (WH Allen, 1973)

2 *Roy Hudd's Cavalcade of Variety Acts – A Who Was Who of Light Entertainment 1945-1960* by Roy Hudd with Philip Hindin (Robson Books, 1997)

3 *Still On My Way To Hollywood* by Ernie Wise (Duckworth, 1990)

4 *Still On My Way To Hollywood* by Ernie Wise (Duckworth, 1990)

5 *There's No Answer To That! An Autobiography* by Eric Morecambe, Ernie Wise and Michael Freedland (Arthur Baker, 1981)

6 *Eric and Ernie – The Autobiography of Morecambe & Wise* by Eric Morecambe, Ernie Wise and Dennis Holman (WH Allen, 1973)

CHAPTER 16: ALAN CURTIS

1 *Eric and Ernie – The Autobiography of Morecambe & Wise* by Eric Morecambe, Ernie Wise and Dennis Holman (WH Allen, 1973)

2 *Still On My Way To Hollywood* by Ernie Wise (Duckworth, 1990)

3 *There's No Answer To That! An Autobiography* by Eric Morecambe, Ernie Wise and Michael Freedland (Arthur Baker, 1981)

4 *Roy Hudd's Cavalcade of Variety Acts – A Who Was Who of Light Entertainment 1945-1960* by Roy Hudd with Philip Hindin (Robson Books, 1997)

CHAPTER 17: STAN STENNETT

1 *Roy Hudd's Cavalcade of Variety Acts – A Who Was Who of Light Entertainment 1945-1960* by Roy Hudd with Philip Hindin (Robson Books, 1997)

CHAPTER 18: BLACKPOOL

1 *Eric and Ernie – The Autobiography of Morecambe & Wise* by Eric Morecambe, Ernie Wise and Dennis Holman (WH Allen, 1973)

2 *Eric and Ernie – The Autobiography of Morecambe & Wise* by Eric Morecambe, Ernie Wise and Dennis Holman (WH Allen, 1973)

3 *Eric and Ernie – The Autobiography of Morecambe & Wise* by Eric Morecambe, Ernie Wise and Dennis Holman (WH Allen, 1973)

4 *Eric and Ernie – The Autobiography of Morecambe & Wise* by Eric Morecambe, Ernie Wise and Dennis Holman (WH Allen, 1973)

5 *Eric and Ernie – The Autobiography of Morecambe & Wise* by Eric Morecambe, Ernie Wise and Dennis Holman (WH Allen, 1973)

6 *Eric and Ernie – The Autobiography of Morecambe & Wise* by Eric Morecambe, Ernie Wise and Dennis Holman (WH Allen, 1973)

CHAPTER 19: GAIL MORECAMBE

1   *Eric and Ernie – The Autobiography of Morecambe & Wise* by Eric Morecambe, Ernie Wise and Dennis Holman (WH Allen, 1973)

CHAPTER 21: FREDDIE DAVIES

1   *Roy Hudd's Cavalcade of Variety Acts – A Who Was Who of Light Entertainment 1945-1960* by Roy Hudd with Philip Hindin (Robson Books, 1997)

CHAPTER 27: MICHAEL GRADE

1   *Roy Hudd's Cavalcade of Variety Acts – A Who Was Who of Light Entertainment 1945-1960* by Roy Hudd with Philip Hindin (Robson Books, 1997)

BIBLIOGRAPHY

Blackpool's Century of Stars by Barry Band (Barry Band, 2002)

The Reluctant Jester by Michael Bentine (Bantam, 1992)

Eric Morecambe Unseen, edited by William Cook (HarperCollins, 2005)

Funny Way To Be A Hero by John Fisher (Frederick Muller, 1973)

Lost Empires – The Phenomenon of Theatres Past, Present and Future by Nigel Fountain
    (Cassell, 2005)

Roy Hudd's Cavalcade of Variety Acts – A Who Was Who of Light Entertainment 1945–960
    by Roy Hudd with Philip Hindin (Robson Books, 1997)

Morecambe & Wise by Graham McCann (Fourth Estate, 1998)

Make 'Em Laugh – Famous Comedians And Their Worlds by Eric Midwinter (George
    Allen and Unwin, 1979)

The People's Jesters – Twentieth Century British Comedians by Eric Midwinter (Third
    Age Press, 2006)

Eric and Ernie – The Autobiography of Morecambe & Wise by Eric Morecambe, Ernie
    Wise and Dennis Holman (WH Allen, 1973)

There's No Answer To That! An Autobiography by Eric Morecambe, Ernie Wise and
    Michael Freedland (Arthur Baker, 1981)

The Straight Man – My Life In Comedy by Nicholas Parsons (Weidenfeld and
    Nicolson, 1994)

Kindly Leave The Stage! The Story of Variety 1919–1960 by Roger Wilmut (Methuen,
    1985)

Still On My Way To Hollywood by Ernie Wise (Duckworth, 1990)

PICTURE CREDITS

Whilst every effort has been made to trace the owners of copyright material reproduced herein, the publishers would like to apologise for any omissions and will be pleased to incorporate missing acknowledgements in any future editions.

3, 11, 61, 173 (top), 222, 225 (ITV/Rex Features); 13 (Harry Myers/Rex Features); 28, 30 (reproduced courtesy of Hazel Smith/Harold Gilderdale/Paul Jenkinson/Gideon Chilton); 31, 91 (London Express/ Hulton Archive/Getty Images); 35, 36, 62–72, 139–41 (reproduced courtesy of Sheila Mathews); 40 (© Edwin Hall); 46, 55 (bottom), 123, 130–2, 163 (reproduced courtesy of Stan Stennett); 57–9 (reproduced courtesy of Doreen Wise); 60 (Everett Collection/Rex Features); 85 (Sylvan Mason/Rex Features); 86 (PhotoPlayUK); 104 (© Bill Wright); 122, 126–8 (reproduced courtesy of Alan Curtis); 125 (© Radio Times); 134 (R. W. Dudley); 136 (Thurston Hopkins/Picture Post/Getty Images); 144 (J. Coleman/N. Charlesworth); 146 (top) (P. A. Reuter Photos Ltd); 168 (top) (© Chic/Daily Express); 168 (bottom) (© Norman Edwards/Evening Despatch); 169 (reproduced courtesy of Freddie Davies); 170 (Brian Moody/Rex Features); 173 (bottom) (Frank Bell/Rex Features); 174, 177 (John Pratt/Hulton Archive/Getty Images); 183–4 (reproduced courtesy of Wyn Calvin); 187 (Alex Dellow/Picture Post/Getty Images); 188 (top)

ABOUT THE AUTHOR

William Cook is the author of *Ha Bloody Ha* (Fourth Estate), *The Comedy Store* (Little, Brown) and *Twenty-Five Years of Viz* (Boxtree). He is the editor of *Tragically I Was An Only Twin – The Complete Peter Cook* (Century), and *Goodbye Again – The Definitive Peter Cook and Dudley Moore* (Century). He also edited *Eric Morecambe Unseen* (HarperCollins). He has worked for the BBC and has written for the *Guardian*, the *Mail on Sunday*, the *New Statesman* and *Condé Nast Traveller*.